T&T CLARK STUDY GUIDES TO THE NEW TESTAMENT

2 CORINTHIANS

Series Editor
Tat-siong Benny Liew, College of the Holy Cross, USA

T0331548

Other titles in the series include:

T&T Clark Study Guides to the Old Testament:

2 CORINTHIANS

An Introduction and Study Guide
Crisis and Conflict

By
Jay Twomey

Bloomsbury T&T Clark
An imprint of Bloomsbury Publishing Plc

B L O O M S B U R Y
LONDON • OXFORD • NEW YORK • NEW DELHI • SYDNEY

Bloomsbury T&T Clark

An imprint of Bloomsbury Publishing Plc

Imprint previously known as T&T Clark

50 Bedford Square
London
WC1B 3DP
UK

1385 Broadway
New York
NY 10018
USA

www.bloomsbury.com

BLOOMSBURY, T&T CLARK and the Diana logo are trademarks of
Bloomsbury Publishing Plc

First published 2013. This edition published 2017

British Library Cataloguing-in-Publication Data
A catalogue record for this book is available from the British Library.

ISBN: PB: 978-0-5676-7119-6
ePDF: 978-0-5676-7121-9
ePub: 978-0-5676-7120-2

Library of Congress Cataloging-in-Publication Data
A catalog record for this book is available from the Library of Congress.

Series: T&T Clark Study Guides to the New Testament, volume 8

Cover design: clareturner.co.uk

Typeset by Jones Ltd, London

CONTENTS

Acknowledgments

This volume is the culmination of an intense but relatively brief period of academic labor. Were it not for the wonderful generosity of the Charles Phelps Taft Research Center at the University of Cincinnati, which granted me a fellowship, freeing me from teaching and other obligations during the 2011-2012 academic year, I probably would not have been able to complete the book on time. I would also like to thank the faculty who were Taft Fellows with me that year for their beneficial advice and support: Donald French, Todd Herzog, Amy Lind, Jenefer Robinson and David Stradling. Tat-Siong Benny Liew was kind enough to invite me to participate in this series and, to him, I owe a debt of gratitude. Finally, the gift of Jackie Knapke's companionship helped to transform the writing process, which can often be tedious, lonely, and frustrating, into a much happier experience than it would have been otherwise. I dedicate the book to her.

ABBREVIATIONS

BHT   Beiträge zur historischen Theologie
FCNT   Feminist Companion to the New Testament and Early Christian
             Writings
HUT   Hermeneutische Untersuchungen zur Theologie
ICC   International Critical Commentary
JSNTSup   *Journal for the Study of the New Testament*, Supplement Series
JSOTSup   *Journal for the Study of the Old Testament*, Supplement Series
KEK   Kritisch-exegetischer Kommentar über das Neue Testament
LNTS   Library of New Testament Studies
NICNT   New International Commentary on the New Testament
NovTSup   Supplements to *Novum Testamentum*
SBLDS   Society of Biblical Literature Dissertation Series
SBLSS   Society of Biblical Literature Symposium Series
SNTMS   Society for New Testament Studies Monograph Series
TNTC   Tyndale New Testament Commentaries
WUNT   Wissenschaftliche Untersuchungen zum Neuen Testament

1

Corinth

It was the best of times, it was the worst of times…

—Charles Dickens, *A Tale of Two Cities*

The Big City

An introduction to critical reflections on Paul's Corinth could easily begin with the epigraph above, the well-known opening of Dickens's *A Tale of Two Cities*. It might even more profitably continue with the rest of that novel's first paragraph, less well-known, which indicates that the opening paradox, while indicative of extremes, refers more specifically to extremes of perspective, or better, to the rhetorical gestures to which such extremes are prone. Ultimately, Dickens explains, the now-elapsed period of best and worst was a lot 'like the present period, [in] that some of its noisiest authorities insisted on its being received, for good or for evil, in the superlative degree of comparison only' (Dickens 2007: 7).

When writing on the Corinthian correspondence, many of our 'authorities', too, have persistently depicted a Corinth in which the best (the Pauline ministry there) struggled valiantly, but perhaps vainly, against the worst (the city in all its sexual and commercial squalor). 'The entire city was like a vast evil resort [*mauvais lieu*], where numerous strangers [or foreigners], above all sailors, went to spend their fortunes foolishly', writes Ernest Renan (1869: 146). 'In a few years', he continues, 'Corinth will present us with a spectacle of incestuous Christians and drunken people seated at the table of Christ', so, consequently, given this licentiousness, 'Paul quickly saw that it would be necessary for him to remain a long while.' More recent descriptions of the city can often describe it in the same tone. Victor Furnish, in his Anchor Bible Commentary, remarks upon 'the generally superficial cultural life of Roman Corinth. Its values were essentially material' (1984: 13, 15). For Furnish, 'This is precisely the kind of setting in which an itinerant philosopher, healer, and fortune-teller' or, worse, a sophist, with his 'noisy claims and shrill accusations', would be welcome; and compared to all this unseemly chaos, Paul's 'style would have seemed as strange as his message'

(1984: 14). As would Paul's religion. Timothy Savage decries the nature of religious life in 'voluptuous' Corinth, a city where the divine functioned not to provide a 'sacred perspective in a secular world', but rather 'to apply a transcendental stamp of approval' to the Corinthian's ruthlessly competitive lives (2004: 48, 51). In more overtly confessional modes, such contrasts can take on an even starker quality, as when Maria Pascuzzi writes that the 'behavior' of Paul's converts, 'still conditioned by Corinth's secular values and aspirations, was destroying God's *ekklēsia*, a microsociety whose unity and holiness were to distinguish it from the macrosociety from which the converts came' (2005: 7).

A growing number of scholars take pains to point out that many commentaries, those guilty of comparisons in the superlative degree, often rely too credulously on prejudicial, and highly exaggerated, ancient characterizations of the moral fiber at Corinth. In these ancient sources, the very name of Corinth could be a byword for illicit sex or prostitution (Adams and Horrell 2004: 7). Jerome Murphy O'Connor has very usefully collected a number of ancient citations relevant to the later scholarly construction of Corinth as a corrupt, shallow, vice-ridden town, even as he doubts 'that the situation there [in Corinth] was any worse than in other port cities of the eastern Mediterranean' (2002: 57). But casting aspersions on Corinth probably has as much, if not more, to do with readings of Paul, as it does with classical texts. It is easy to see why this is so, especially if one takes Paul's own texts as one's (ideally transparent and completely accurate) point of departure. In addition to the passage Renan has in mind about incest (1 Cor. 5.1), for example, Paul also must address more general concerns about 'sexual immorality' (1 Cor. 5.11; 7.2; 10.8), as well as 'impurity ... licentiousness' (2 Cor. 12.21) and fornication with prostitutes (1 Cor. 6.13-18). Then there's the problem of drunkenness in table fellowship, or at least a selfish indulgence (1 Cor. 11.20-22), as well as: factionalism (1 Cor. 1.10-13; 3.3-4, 21; 11.18-19; 2 Cor. 10–13); litigiousness (1 Corinthians 6); greed, idolatry, revilement, theft (1 Cor. 5.11); partnerships with the unrighteous (2 Cor. 6.14-18, cf. 1 Cor. 7.12-16); divisive competition (1 Corinthians 12–14; 2 Cor. 11.21-29), sometimes involving mercenary or predatory mission tactics (2 Cor. 11.20), and so on. So, given all this, along with the generally dubious reputation of Corinth among ancient writers, *why not* agree with the characterizations of Renan and others?

The work of feminist, queer and postcolonial scholars, any readers engaging a hermeneutics of suspicion, suggests that the answer has as much to do with historical data as with the social and political ramifications of that data's interpretations. As Amy-Jill Levine has put it, no one 'come[s] to Paul's texts as innocents .... Our cultures, and so we, are heirs to Paul's legacy', a legacy derived not just from the Pauline corpus, but also, and much more significantly, from the history of Pauline interpretation, so that 'to respond to Paul is also to respond to all those who have been and continue to be influenced by him' (2004: 2). And of course, everyone influenced by Paul is also, at the same time, rooted in, and motivated by, specific historical and ideological contexts, so that Paul is always the Paul—or, as Richard Walsh likes to say, the 'Pauls' (2005: 8)—of those contexts as well. The more willing we are to acknowledge that our lenses are also sometimes blinders, the more conscious we are of our own motivations and how they jibe or clash with others precisely on the basis of the ideological predispositions involved, the more sensitive, innovative and productive our interpretations will be.

What about Corinth, then? For some scholars it is not enough simply to say that Corinth was more complicated than earlier commentators allow. In fact, at various moments in this book we will see how readers' emphases on the lived complexity of Corinth, on the kinds of things Paul and the members of his community are likely to have seen and experienced in their daily lives in the city, can have the effect of making Corinth seem less like the Slough of Despond and rather more like many of the cities we ourselves know. That is, despite the very significant distance and differences between Paul's Corinth and our twenty-first-century urban experiences, Corinth was still a place of aspirations, tensions, desires, of identities merging or clashing in public and private, of orders and relationships social and political. Or, reversing our focus, we might very simply note that a view of pre-Pauline Corinthian religion such as Timothy Savage's, quoted above, can easily apply to our own world. Is it not true, after all, that the most ostentatiously religious of the two major US political parties is also the most fully in cahoots with capitalism in its rawest forms? Similarly, and more positively, can one not describe many of our largest cities almost precisely in the way Calvin Roetzel describes Roman Corinth, as 'a multiethnic and multinational collection of skilled [men] and women' (2007: 20)? Or consider the way Stanley Stowers describes people like Paul, as skilled individuals 'without ties to the land and who lived lives characterized by physical mobility', people dwelling 'in a polyethnic world with a predilection toward transcending their ascribed local and ethnic places' (2011: 139). Surely something in these characterizations rings a contemporary bell. And, if so, then one might actually want to go much further than merely underlining potential similarities between Paul's Corinth and our world as a way of undoing previous critical prejudices. With a scholar like Richard Horsley, for instance, one could even try to invalidate the older view entirely by arguing that the 'riff-raff' populating Corinth constituted a potential political threat to the powers that be under the 'warlord Julius Caesar', making Paul's work among them seem akin to radical labor organizing or anti-colonial struggle: 'Paul and his co-workers were building a movement, not saving souls or founding a religion' (2009: 222, 225-26). As will become clear in the rest of this volume, I am quite sympathetic to readings such as Horsley's. Here at the outset, however, it's simply important to be aware (and wary) of the use of easy polarities in the treatment of our evidence, especially when much of that evidence—including Paul's own rhetoric—is just as likely as the scholarship focused upon it to be motivated as well.

Still, we can run through the basic information about this city, which Paul made a temporary home and where he faced some of the most interesting, to us at least, challenges of his career, relatively quickly. The Greek city, about which the sources alluded to above mostly speak, was not the Corinth Paul knew. Ancient Corinth was devastated in 146 BCE by the troops under Roman consul Lucius Mummius, who brought a decisive end to the Achaean League. Although the site was probably occupied to some extent during the century following the Achaean War, it wasn't until after 44 BCE, when Julius Caesar installed a Roman colony at Corinth, that the city became a thriving center once again, populated, at least initially, by freed slaves hailing from Syria, Egypt, Palestine and other parts of the eastern Mediterranean. Given its location on an isthmus and the city's two ports (Lechaeum and Cenchreae), it is often noted that Corinth had a strong commercial dimension to it. Culturally it was also significant, however, as, among other things, the host of the Isthmian Games, a major athletic (and religio-cultural) festival held every two years—including once in 51 CE, when there is a good chance that Paul was resident in Corinth. As one would expect for any such urban center, there were theaters, multiple shrines and temples (dedicated, for instance, to Asclepius [the god of healing], to Aphrodite, to the imperial cult and so on) and a forum complex. An inscription on a lintel, discovered in the late nineteenth century, also points to the existence of a synagogue in Corinth. While it is tempting to imagine that it might have belonged to the synagogue Luke describes Paul visiting in Acts 18, most scholars assume that the inscription—which read 'Synagogue of the Hebrews'—comes from a time well after Paul.

When Was That, Exactly?

As mentioned above, we will return later to a handful of more granular descriptions of daily life in Corinth during Paul's time. But what time was Paul's time, exactly? And when was Paul in Corinth, and for how long? Typically, New Testament texts divulge few historical cues, and this is true of Paul's letters as well. Scholars will generally refer to Acts only cautiously in reconstructing early Christian history, given the differences between Luke's account and Paul's own letters, not to mention the historical priority of

Paul. But in some instances, Luke's text is similar enough to Paul's to allow for speculative reconstructions of chronology. Both Paul and Luke mention Paul's escape from Damascus, for example. In 2 Cor. 11.32-33, Paul recounts how, being 'let down in a basket through a window in the wall', he fled from the 'governor [or ethnarch] under King Aretas'. Acts 9 indicates that this event, although it is described rather differently by Luke, took place at the start of Paul's ministry. The nature and dating of the Nabatean King Aretas's authority over Damascus are disputed, but, if it is at least remotely possible that Paul's memory is accurate, then this incident could have occurred as late as 40 CE, the year of Aretas's death. The situation of Paul's stay in Corinth is likewise aided by certain similarities with Luke, although, again, it is difficult to be reliably specific. Paul visits Corinth in Acts 18. Silas and Timothy are his colleagues in that text, as in Paul's letters, where Silas is called Silvanus (2 Cor. 1.19). Luke indicates that Paul meets Aquila and his wife Priscilla, who had left Rome after Claudius's expulsion of the Jews (49 CE), in Corinth. This couple is mentioned by Paul in 1 Cor. 16.19 as well as in Romans 16.3 (see also 2 Tim. 4.19) where Priscilla, or Prisca as Paul calls her, is named first. Incidentally, other figures of significance to Corinth, and who make appearances both in Acts and Paul, are Apollos (Acts 18.24–19.1; 1 Cor. 1.12; 16.12), Crispus (Acts 18.8; 1 Cor. 1.14) and perhaps Sosthenes (Acts 18.17; 1 Cor. 1.1). Paul also mentions Erastus, 'the city treasurer', in the greetings section of Romans (16.23; cf. Acts 19.22), which was probably written from Cenchreae, Corinth's port. There is independent archaeological evidence, in the form of an inscription, of a well-to-do individual named Erastus, who was 'in effect a commissioner of public works' (Furnish 1984: 25). While the inscription cannot easily be dated, it is not impossible that this Erastus and Paul's are one and the same. Ben Witherington, adopting a social-scientific approach, considers the identity especially likely because Paul, if he were a Roman citizen from a good family, 'would have naturally identified with those ... who were socially better off' (1995: 32). Needless to say, such a view of Paul's class preferences is not universally held, but there is no reason to doubt that Erastus might have been counted among those who were 'powerful' or 'of noble birth' in his community (1 Cor. 1.26). An additional, very important Lukan reference, missing from Paul, is to Gallio, whom we know to have been 'proconsul of Achaia' (Acts 18.12) for a year in 51–52 CE. After narrating a public crisis overseen (if largely ignored) by Gallio, Luke indicates that Paul departed from Corinth, sailing from Cenchreae initially for Ephesus, ultimately reaching Antioch, at the end of his second missionary journey (Acts 18.18-22). Taking this information as a basic starting point, it would seem that Paul probably arrived in Corinth for the first time in 50 CE. This would give Prisca and Aquila time to have resettled there after leaving Rome in 49 CE, and it allows for Luke's claims that Paul spent a year and a half in Corinth before his departure (Acts 18.11) and that he left while Gallio was still on the scene.

So far so good. Knottier chronological problems arise when we turn to the question of when Paul wrote his Corinthian correspondence. While a complicated reading of Acts 18 as a composite text recording different visits would allow for an initial stay in Corinth as early as 41 CE (Lüdemann 1984: 159, 262), most scholars, following the timeline given above, assume that 1 Corinthians must have been written after 52 CE. Paul indicates that sometime subsequent to his departure from Corinth, yet prior to his penning of 1 Corinthians, he both wrote a letter (1 Cor. 5.9), now lost, and received emissaries and at least one letter from the community there (1 Cor. 1.11; 7.1). Given the slow pace of ancient travel and communications, it is clear that some time will necessarily have passed in the interval. For a variety of specific additional reasons—including especially the New Testament evidence regarding Paul's long Ephesian ministry (1 Cor. 16.8; cf. Acts 19), as well as suppositions about Timothy's possible itinerary as he journeyed from Ephesus to Corinth and back—the majority opinion is that 1 Corinthians was dispatched a couple of years after Paul's initial Corinthian stay, in 54 CE or thereabouts.

The dating of 2 Corinthians is even trickier, since there are no specific historical markers to rely upon and the integrity of the letter in its canonical form is doubtful. We will discuss various ways of construing the letter and its component parts in the next chapter. For now, we can limit ourselves to some brief reflections. At the end of 1 Corinthians, Paul announces that he would like to revisit Corinth 'after passing through Macedonia' (16.5). 2 Corinthians begins with evidence of a dispute between Paul and the Corinthian community stemming, in part, from Paul's failure to make the promised visit. He may have skipped his planned return because he wanted to avoid a repeat of a different, more recent, unannounced 'painful visit' to Corinth (2.1). Or, instead of a double visit (1.15-16, 23), on his way to and from Macedonia, Paul may have visited only the first time, encountering difficulties and refusing to return as promised (Barrett 1973: 7-8, 86; cf. Downs 2008: 45-47; Fee 2001: 104; Thrall 1994: 74). Either way, after the troubling visit, he wrote another letter, often referred to in the scholarship as the tearful letter (see 2.4), and quite possibly sent by Titus's hand. This, at least the third of Paul's Corinthian letters, is either to be found in 2 Corinthians 10–13 or is lost to us. Paul himself then set out from Ephesus to Macedonia (2.12-13; Acts 20.1-3), where he reconnected finally with Titus (7.5-6), learned that the tearful letter had successfully salvaged his bond with the Corinthians (7.7-16), and wrote our document. How long would all of this have taken? The most thorough considerations of the possibilities suggest that Paul could have made his painful visit within the year after the writing of 1 Corinthians, especially if Timothy had rushed back to Ephesus from Corinth (see 1 Cor. 4.17; 16.10) to alert him of trouble brewing there. Assuming that another year would be required for an intermediate visit, Titus's journey and Paul's trip to Macedonia, one may suppose, very tentatively, that 2 Corinthians was written in 55-56 CE. If, as many scholars believe, 2 Corinthians 10–13 is not part of the original letter, and if these chapters do not consist of the earlier letter of tears, but instead preserve a fragment of a later letter, written after Paul learned of yet another crisis in his relationship with the community in Corinth, then one must posit an additional stretch of time, perhaps another year, which would bring us quite possibly to 57 CE.

2

The Composition of 2 Corinthians

Now I appeal to you ... that there be no divisions.

1 Cor. 1.10

A Matter of Integrity

Descriptions of Corinth and chronological reconstructions of Paul's relationship with the Corinthians can engender disagreements, as we have seen, but they tend to be fairly limited in scope. When it comes to characterizing the literary integrity of our letter, on the other hand, it is much harder to reach a consensus. There is a variety of interpretive options on the table, ranging from the simplest (2 Corinthians is a single, coherent letter) to the most complex (2 Corinthians consists of up to nine independent component parts). In my view, 2 Corinthians is a composite text, consisting of at least two major segments from independent letters (2 Corinthians 1–9; 2 Corinthians 10–13). Other portions of the epistle may also be fragments or separate documents, and we will examine these passages in turn. It used to be, as Jerome Murphy-O'Connor notes, that 'the majority of scholars believed [2 Corinthians] to be a compilation of at least two letters. The unity of [2 Corinthians] still had its faithful defenders, however, and in recent years they have grown in number to the point where unity now appears to be the majority opinion' (2010: 160). Even if that is a slight exaggeration, a growing number of scholars does, indeed, accept the integrity of the letter, and this has much to do with the ongoing significance of rhetorical studies in New Testament scholarship. In what follows, we will first examine various partition theories. We'll begin with the simplest two-letter hypotheses, which try to articulate the relationship between 2 Corinthians 1–9 and 2 Corinthians 10–13. A significant dimension of our discussion of this basic partition model will involve considering the possibility that 2 Corinthians 10–13 is the letter of tears mentioned in 2 Cor. 2.4. This, in turn, will lead to more complicated partition theories, necessitating distinct discussions of the function and chronological (dis)placement of 2 Corinthians 8 and 9, as well as 2 Cor. 2.14–7.4 and 6.14–7.1. Next, we will focus on unity theories.

Using classical rhetorical categories, these theories attempt, with varying degrees of success, to explain how 2 Corinthians functions as an intelligible compositional unity from start to finish. In general, the less rigid the reliance upon classical forms in these attempts, the more successful the analysis. Some unity theorists, however, do not take a rhetorical approach at all, and we will conclude the chapter with a look at these options.

A Letter of Parts?

Partition theories have been the dominant way of construing 2 Corinthians' irregularities since the late eighteenth century. As you might expect, they depend upon both chronological reconstructions (such as the one outlined above) and related considerations of the most likely sequence of letters or letter fragments within 2 Corinthians, even given that that sequence cannot be dated very adequately. The major division between 2 Corinthians 1–9 and 10–13 is usually the first point of departure in any examination of the letter as a composite text, and this is due to a prominent feature of 2 Corinthians itself. For how can one fail to notice the abrupt shift in tone between 2 Corinthians 1–9 and 2 Corinthians 10–13? The earlier chapters give evidence of some sort of conflict(s) between Paul and the community, it is true, but the tone there is largely one of reconciliation. Paul expresses his 'great pride' (7.4) in the church, he rejoices in his 'comfort' and 'consolation' (7.13) now that the rift is healing and he assures his correspondents that they have his 'complete confidence' (7.16). In 2 Corinthians 10, however, Paul is suddenly astringent: 'I ask that when I am present I need not show boldness by daring to oppose those who think we are acting according to human standards' (10.2). He goes on to refer to his critics as satanic (11.14-15), considers the whole enterprise of needing to respond to them a kind of madness (11.23), and concludes by saying that he 'will not be lenient' (13.2) when he comes again, that, in fact, he may need to be quite 'severe' (13.10). A further noticeable difference is that, in 2 Corinthians 1–9, the first person plural predominates, whereas, in 2 Corinthians 10–13, Paul uses 'I' much more frequently, contributing to the reader's experience of an epistolary break. Adding 2 Corinthians 8–9 into the mix only complicates matters further, for why should Paul follow his request for a resumption (8.6; cf. 1 Cor. 16.1-4) of the collection for the saints in those chapters with a long section of scathing polemic and ironic apologia? One possible answer, clearly, is that he never did any such thing.

The tonal rupture starting at 2 Corinthians 10 probably flags a textual rupture, or rather a redactional suture, fusing two very different texts and confusing their chronology. Unfortunately for partition theories, there is no evidence in the history of interpretation that 2 Corinthians ever circulated as multiple, independent texts requiring later redaction to achieve their, or its, present form. The earliest witnesses to the Christian textual tradition do not reference the letter, meaning that there was a significant period during which the redaction might have been effected. From Marcion, in the mid-second century onward, though, 2 Corinthians has been considered canonical, but, again, in its present form. Those who hold to one or another partition theory do not put serious stock in arguments from the silent, murky origins of the text. Rather, on the basis of evidence internal to the letter, they try to re-imagine Paul's experience in Corinth.

If 2 Corinthians 1–7/8/9 precede 2 Corinthians 10–13, this means that after salving wounds and repairing relations with the Corinthians, hostilities of a vaguely similar sort broke out afresh later. Margaret Thrall argues that 2 Corinthians 1–8 was followed shortly by 2 Corinthians 9 and then 2 Corinthians 10–13 (2000: 503, 566). We will see below that 2 Corinthians 8 and 9 may also need to be displaced, hence my ambivalence in designating which chapter concludes the first major portion of 2 Corinthians. Additionally, since Paul's final letter, Romans, concludes with greetings sent from Cenchreae, it would appear that, after writing 2 Corinthians 10–13, Paul once again re-established ties with his Corinthian church. Surely, if anyone were ever up to riding this rollercoaster of crisis and reconciliation, it would be Paul. Nevertheless, some scholars would prefer a less convoluted history. What if 2 Corinthians 10–13 were the letter of tears, they ask? In that case, the simmering challenges to Pauline authority and theology attested in 1 Corinthians would have boiled over into a direct conflict between the writing of that earlier letter and 2 Corinthians 1–7/8/9. Paul's abortive visit would then have eventuated in a letter of tears, now preserved in, or as, our 2 Corinthians 10–13, which turned the tide of opinion once again towards Paul, leading him, finally, to write his conciliatory letter and to revisit Corinth for a stay long enough to compose and send Romans.

The internal evidence for this view is not entirely compelling to the majority of partition theorists, but it is worth considering fully. First, Paul writes, in 12.14 and 13.1-2, that he is now planning a third visit, and that he hopes things have changed since his second visit, when he warned 'those who sinned and all the others' that he would 'not be lenient'. If the second visit were the painful visit (2.1), then the third visit could be his final stay in Corinth (Rom. 16.1).

Second, it is frequently noted that, in 2 Corinthians 10–13, the opponents are plural and outsiders—Paul dismisses them, satirically, as 'super apostles' (11.5; 12.11) who have come 'proclaim[ing] another Jesus' (11.4)—whereas the now-resolved conflict, in 2 Corinthians 1–7/8/9, concerns a single individual who might have attacked Paul personally, rather than on theological grounds (2.5-8). Moreover, in 2.9, Paul says that he 'wrote for this reason', implying that the tearful letter dealt specifically with that individual. For readers down the centuries, this has brought to mind the challenge Paul addressed in 1 Corinthians 5, the case of a man sleeping with his widowed step-mother. Some in the community had approved of this man's behavior, and, in response, Paul both upbraided the community and demanded a course of punishment. The similarities are interesting but not satisfying. For one thing, in the earlier letter, Paul prescribes an apparently permanent punishment (5.4-5, 13), while, in 2 Cor. 2.5, the punishment seems to have been devised by the community, and Paul now asks them to relent and forgive the individual. Taking seriously the identity of the two situations would also imply that 1 Corinthians is, itself, the letter of tears, a reading no longer widely credited (but see Long 2004). After all, the integrity of 1 Corinthians is not in question, the letter itself is hardly a letter of tears, and the many problems addressed there indicate that Paul was speaking to different individuals, or groups of individuals, about a variety of rather unrelated questions. Returning to our text, then, while the different sources of opposition in 2 Corinthians 1–7/8/9 (an individual) and 2 Corinthians 10–13 (a group of outsiders) suggest to many that the latter cannot be the letter of tears, some argue, to the contrary, that both documents are related to the same general crisis involving, in both cases, a specific person. Most scholars would agree with David Horrell, for instance, who notes that the Greek in 10.7 ('If anyone [masculine singular] is confident that *he* belongs to Christ'), in 10.10 ('For *he* says') and in 10.11 ('Let such a person [masculine singular] understand'), although rendered as plurals in English translations, such as the NRSV, at least potentially hints that 'a particular person may be in mind' in these chapters, as in 2 Corinthians 2 (1996: 308; cf. Roetzel 2007: 136). Most scholars would also go on to say that, in actual practice, such generic referents may be either plural or singular. While this is true, it is still not impossible that Paul has an individual in mind, perhaps the individual who, to spite him, opted to welcome and provide a platform for the pesky itinerant 'super apostles' (Horrell 1996: 222; also Barrett 1973: 291).

Third, in 2 Corinthians 10–13, Paul seems to respond to accusations of financial improprieties, probably pertaining to the collection (8.16-18), which led to a suspension of fundraising activities on the part of the Corinthians (8.6). In 8.16-24, however, Paul, now sensitive to these charges, can be understood to have adjusted his *modus operandi* as part of his reconciliation effort.

Finally, it could be that taking 2 Corinthians 10–13 as the letter of tears contributes, more elegantly than other theories, to the solution of uncertainties in reading 2 Corinthians. One of these uncertainties involves Paul's apparently inexplicable detour into an exegesis of Exod. 34.29-35 (among other texts) in 2 Corinthians 3. As many propose, the opponents in 2 Corinthians 10–13 may be competing with Paul on the grounds of a shared Jewish heritage (11.22-23), quite possibly by encouraging an interest in their own idiosyncratic use of, or arguments about, scriptural tradition (10.5). The reading of Moses in 2 Corinthians 3, coming after the letter of tears had dispatched the most urgent issues, might now more comprehensibly be contextualized as a response to a more neutral area of disagreement. Similarly, the reference to letters of recommendation (3.1) might be clearer if we were to take Paul's earlier, intense agitation over the self-commendation and boasting of the opponents (10.8, 12, 13, 15-18; 11.12-13, 16-18, 21, 30; 12.1, 5, 6, 9) as background. And Laurence Welborn has shown that, even if none of these issues crops up very directly in 2 Corinthians 1–7/8/9, that in itself is no argument against reading 2 Corinthians 10–13 as the letter of tears, since ancient letters of reconciliation, being politely conciliatory, typically did not risk abrading wounds on the mend by addressing such particulars (1995).

Besides those mentioned in the course of the preceding discussion, some common contemporary objections to reading 2 Corinthians 10–13 as the tearful letter are that this text doesn't mention the painful visit, which was its immediate inspiration, nor is there any indication that Paul advocated a punishment for the wrongdoer. One might reply, speculatively of course, that 2 Corinthians 10–13 is only part of the letter of tears, or that the punishment was an innovation on the part of the Corinthians themselves. More importantly, critics point to a discrepancy between 2 Corinthians 8–9 and 2 Corinthians 10–13 regarding the activity of Titus. In 12.17-18, Paul refers to a past visit of Titus's, presumably with regard to the collection mentioned in 2 Corinthians 8–9. But, in 8.6, 16–9.5, Titus's visit is still projected for the future. To many, the future of 2 Corinthians 8–9 is the past of 2 Corinthians 12, necessarily making 2 Corinthians 10–13 a later document. K.L. McKay (1995) has argued that it is possible to construe the relevant verbs in 8.17-18 as historical aorists, as 'went' and 'sent with', rather than 'is going' and 'are sending', respectively, which would indicate that Titus had been sent already, prior to the writing of 2 Corinthians 8. A reading of this sort could help to align 2 Corinthians 8 and 12. Nevertheless, most scholars, and especially those who do not consider 2 Corinthians 10–13 to be the letter of tears, take these verbs as epistolary aorists, which indicate a future action, from Paul's perspective, but one that will have been completed by the time the letter is read (e.g. see Harris 2005: 600, 891; Matera 2003: 194, 297; Thrall 2000: 547, 854-57; Barrett 1973: 228, 325; see also Murphy-O'Connor 1998; Witherington 1995). An additional factor pertaining to this material is that, in 2 Corinthians 8, Paul refers to two anonymous brothers who will accompany Titus, whereas, in 12.17-18, only one brother is mentioned. The uncertainty as to what this difference means seems generally irrelevant to one's reconstruction of 2 Corinthians, however, especially when scholars with opposed views on the chronological placement of 2 Corinthians 10–13 can draw precisely the same conclusions about the brother of 12.18 (as do Furnish 1984: 566 and Roetzel 2007: 116).

The temporal disjunction between the two major segments of 2 Corinthians might be resolved if 2 Corinthians 8 happened to have been written earlier than the rest of the letter, in fact immediately following 1 Corinthians. If this were the case, one could imagine a context in which an early letter of tears might refer back less problematically to Titus's visit. Such an intriguing interpretive option, which leads us beyond the pale of our two-letter hypothesis, is advanced by Margaret Mitchell, who reconstructs 2 Corinthians as follows: (1) Paul writes 2 Corinthians 8 from Macedonia after completing the canonical 1 Corinthians and entertaining the Corinthian responses and after skipping his promised next visit to Corinth. This letter (2 Corinthians 8) provokes an angry reply, not least because Paul uses it to authorize his own envoys for the collection rather than deferring to the Corinthians, as he had said he would do in 1 Cor. 16.3-4; (2) Paul then defends himself with another letter, sometimes called 'a first apology', contained in 2.14–7.4, after writing which he visits Corinth only to be rebuffed there, perhaps by an individual who contrasted Paul unfavorably with the example of other apostles, like Apollos or Cephas; (3) retreating to Ephesus, Paul 'crafts a bitter and intensely clever argument' that takes shape as 2 Corinthians 10–13; (4) eventually, Paul meets up with Titus in Macedonia, learns about an incipient reconciliation and writes a letter of reconciliation consisting of our 2 Cor. 1.1–2.13; 7.5-16; 13.11-13; (5) finally, Paul kick-starts the collection again with what is now 2 Corinthians 9 (Mitchell 2010: 7-8; 2005: 333-35; cf. Roetzel 2007; for a concise, but detailed, survey of the critical pre-history of complex partition theories such as these, see the introduction in Vegge 2008: 12-22). Separating 2 Corinthians 8 from 2 Corinthians 9 in this 'virtually unprecedented' way also takes into account the peculiar redundancy of the two, and of which 9.1 seems oblivious (Mitchell 2005: 324-25). There, Paul writes, 'Now it is not necessary for me to write about the ministry to the saints', when he's been writing about nothing else for the last twenty-four verses. It should be noted that Stanley Stowers has argued that the opening of 2 Corinthians 9, in fact, builds upon 2 Corinthians 8 by means of emphasis through repetition, but that the argument is pressed in a manner that is politely attentive to the recipients' sensibilities (1990; but see the hesitation regarding this suggestion in Thrall 2000: 564).

An alternative rearrangement of the two chapters would be that of Hans Dieter Betz, against whom Stowers argues. Betz proposes that both 2 Corinthians 8 and 9 were written after 2 Corinthians 10–13; they were last in the series of letters and were sent as separate epistles to slightly different audiences (2 Corinthians 8 to Corinth and 2 Corinthians 9 to Achaia more generally). It is true that Corinth is technically part of Achaia, but, Betz argues, Paul needed assistance in rallying the Corinthians to the completion of their collection efforts (1985: 93; cf. Georgi 1991: 93). According to Betz, Paul is alerting the other Achaian churches generally to the possibility of the Corinthian failure. So, Romans 15.26 is important to the argument. Achaia's contribution to the collection would include that of Corinth. If Corinth did not follow through, then Paul *and* Achaia would be humiliated (9.4). It is unclear, however, why 2 Corinthians 9 should not be more direct, if this reading is valid. Achaia might have been mentioned in 9.2 merely for the parallelism with Macedonia (so Furnish 1984: 431), or because Paul knows that he is addressing not only Corinth, but also affiliated churches in the region (Barrett 1973: 55-56; cf. 1 Cor. 16.15). But, whatever Paul's reason, most readers assume that both 2 Corinthians 8 and 2 Corinthians 9 were addressed to Corinth.

Finally, we need to consider two remaining segments of 2 Corinthians with which partition theories typically deal (2.14–7.4 and 6.14–7.1) before turning to readings of the letter as a unified whole. According to the two-letter hypothesis, 2 Corinthians 1–7 (or 1–7/8/9) constitutes a letter of reconciliation, one building upon a nascent goodwill towards Paul, after the latter had criticized the community in Corinth, perhaps too harshly (2.2; 7.8). The extent of the reconciliation is less of an issue than the contours of the letter of reconciliation itself. A major section of this letter, from 2.14–7.4, seems so significant a digression from Paul's otherwise coherent narrative about his reunion with Titus in Macedonia (7.5 picks up where 2.13 had left off, according to this view) that many scholars cited above (including Mitchell) think it might also have belonged to a different missive. While this may certainly be the case, the fact remains that (with the exception discussed below) one can read over the apparent epistolary seams quite easily. Perhaps, then, 2.14–7.4 is not an interpolated letter at all, but rather a fully Pauline digression in context (e.g. Hubbard 2004: 134)? Furnish takes this sensible logic further and argues that only the later exegete, curious to know more about Paul's encounter with Titus, would see a break here. Paul's audience, he says, fully aware, or fully capable, of picturing the whole of that backstory, was much more interested in Paul's reaction to Titus's message, and this is exactly what they get in 2 Corinthians 1–7 (1984: 391).

Still, even 2 Corinthians 1–7/8/9 bears evidence of an interpolation in 6.14–7.1. Since the early nineteenth century, 6.14–7.1 has seemed to many scholars to be an odd text, possibly even a non-Pauline interpolation (see the overview in Thrall 1994: 25-36). There is an obvious continuity between 6.12 and 7.2 in Paul's appeal to the Corinthians that they 'open their hearts' to him. Apparently interrupting this continuity is a fragment about strict separation from 'unbelievers' (6.14), supported by a catena of citations (from Leviticus, Ezekiel, Isaiah and 2 Samuel), and concluding with a call for spiritual and bodily purity. Scholars frequently note the un-Pauline language, including the reference to Satan as Beliar (6.15). That allusion, as well as the strong dualism of the text, has suggested the influence of, or an origin in, Qumran, even though similar language and contrasts are to be found in other extra-canonical texts, such as the *Testament of Levi* (19.1). If 6.14–7.1 is an interpolation, then, it may reflect the exegesis and perspective of Paul's opponents (Gunther 1973: 313). Alternatively, it has been proposed that this is a genuine Pauline fragment, perhaps even from his earliest letter (1 Cor. 5.9-13 would be a partially clarifying response to some Corinthian misreading of this passage). But because none of these solutions has proven entirely satisfactory, there is a general trend in most recent work to try to comprehend the passage within its current context, even if its authenticity is deemed uncertain. To cite just one example, Paul Duff, who imagines that Paul himself may be the redactor responsible for our interpolation, argues very interestingly that the passage is consonant with the larger epistolary context, which involves the imagery of processions (2.14). He conjectures that the heart motif in 6.13 and 7.2 would call to mind the herald at an epiphany procession, asking the Corinthians to make way for God's entry. Heralds in cultic processions often had as a key task the separation of the initiate from the uninitiated. Thus, as the fragment calls out for separation from unbelievers, and as the context seems to depict Paul as a herald leading a procession to the temple of the deity (in this case, the Christian community itself), Paul, or a redactor, found that it was sensible to add the fragment precisely here (Duff 1993).

A Seamless Whole?

Where does all this leave us? Not, it would seem, with the elegant two-letter hypothesis with which we began. Yet the interpretive acrobatics required in making allowances for each and every possible letter fragment in 2 Corinthians may be unappealing as well. Partly for this reason, one suspects, theories of the epistle's unity have been gaining ground of late. Actually, 're-gaining ground' would be a better way of putting it, because efforts to establish the unity of 2 Corinthians, and possibly to justify the traditional reading, have always arisen in response to partition theories (Betz 1985: 27). The current burst of critical energy owes a great deal to the growing significance of rhetorical studies of New Testament texts. More precisely, the study of ancient rhetorical genres—as opposed to another important branch of research focusing on the politics of Paul's own rhetoric (e.g. Castelli 1991 or Schüssler Fiorenza 2007)—has encouraged advocates of unity to understand the letter's seams and fissures otherwise, that is, as markers of transitions within one or another standard classical form, or, more generally, as indications of the continuity of Paul's thought in the letter on the basis of parallels with classical rhetorical strategies. Rhetorical criticism is useful in partition theories as well (e.g. Betz 1985; Welborn 1995), but unity theories have made the most extensive use of rhetoric in discussing the integrity of 2 Corinthians.

Among the more recent formal rhetorical studies of the letter's unity is Fredrick Long's *Ancient Rhetoric and Paul's Apology* (2004). Long, building upon and engaging with similar work by Witherington (1995), Young and Ford (1987) and Betz (1972), argues that, in 2 Corinthians, we have a complete example of an apology, an instance of forensic speech which has a clear 'rhetorical disposition', by which he means 'the intentional arrangement of the speech according to conventional sections which attempts best to foster favorable attention and persuasion in the audience' (Long 2004: 71). The different sections, which Long finds in any number of ancient parallels from Cicero, Quintilian and others, are as follows: *prooemium* (1.3-7), or an opening statement; *narratio* (1.8-16; 2.12-13; 7.2-16), an outline of the basic situation behind the case; *divisio* and *partitio* (1.17-24), an articulation of the allegations; *probatio* (2.1–9.15), the rebuttal of allegations; *refutatio* (10.1–11.15), an attack upon the accusers, usually only tangentially related to the allegations; self-adulation (11.16–12.10), the defense's praiseful assessment of his own character; and *peroratio* (12.11–13.10), a concluding summation (Long 2004: 143-98). The virtue of Long's work—and any similarly structured reading of the unity of 2 Corinthians—is that it can account for each apparently distinct segment of the letter. The problems with such readings, however, are many. One of the most basic ones, in Long's case, for example, is that the charges against Paul, recapitulated in 2 Corinthians 1, focus on Paul's failure to visit as promised and his reliance upon worldly motives, or acting *kata sarka* ('according to the flesh'). This means, specifically, that everything in the apology needs to respond to these charges and their implications. Paul's discussion of the collection, in 2 Corinthians 8–9, and his apparently related defensive questions about fiscal propriety in 2 Corinthians 12, thus need to stem entirely from the accusation in 1.17b about his making plans according to human standards (Long 2004: 127, 178). When Paul turns directly to the charge of operating *kata sarka* in the *refutation* (10.1–11.15), however, his concern is evidently about the legitimacy of his ministry, which he avers has a divine source. There is nothing at this point in the letter about 'financial trickery' (Long 2004: 129). Long's reliance upon an ancient forensic paradigm reduces a great deal of the variety and complexity of 2 Corinthians, not to mention much of Paul's own heated rhetoric, to an exegesis of half a verse in the first chapter, which, according to most commentators, concerns only the problem of the changed itinerary (e.g. Roetzel 2007: 132-33; Harris 2005: 196-98; Matera 2003: 52-54; Thrall 1994: 140-43; Furnish 1984: 141-45). This is not to say that Long's readings of specific issues aren't valuable. But his interpretation overall, and others like his, can frequently seem arbitrary or forced.

If even Quintilian, an 'admirable spokesman for common sense', insisted upon flexibility and creativity (i.e. bending, if not breaking, the rules of rhetoric), then why should rhetorical criticism restrict Paul's writings to detailed models found in a rhetor's handbook (Murphy-O'Connor 2010: 165)? And many scholars of Pauline rhetoric want to insist that Paul's style in 2 Corinthians is more spontaneously fluid than someone like Long would allow. An extreme example of this alternative approach is David R. Hall's image: rather than seeing the apostle as a careful rhetorical craftsman, we should recognize that 'he was more like a dog being taken for a walk, who is distracted first by one scent and then by another' (2003: 122)—which is striking, to say the least. Unfortunately, Hall's evocative characterization hardly explains the differences between the Corinthian letters. Both, undoubtedly, are '"mixed" letters [of] several sections, each with its own rhetorical structure' (Hall 2003: 119), rather than full forensic speeches, say, in epistolary form. But 1 Corinthians has a logical and rhetorical forward motion that 2 Corinthians lacks. It is possible that the major tonal adjustment in 2 Cor. 10.1 is due to the fact that Paul now takes up the pen and defends himself against personal attacks, whereas, earlier in the letter, he had been participating in a collective effort (Hall 2003: 112). Nevertheless, one needs to come up with adequate reasons as to why the 'I myself, Paul' of 10.1 is so much more abrupt than in other similarly personal moments in the Pauline corpus (e.g. Gal. 5.2; Rom. 15.14; Phlm 1.19).

A more nuanced rhetorically based reading of the epistle's unity is that of Ivar Vegge, who rightly points out how readers of 2 Corinthians sometimes fail to notice that the so-called letter of reconciliation is still fraught with crisis. The full resolution at 2 Cor. 7.16 is often taken at face value, even though the very problem resolved here—concerning 'the one who did the wrong' (7.12)—is still being worked out in 2.5-11. The crisis clearly involves different parties, a 'majority' (2.6) and an individual who has been punished, but is still backed, perhaps, by a minority, possibly those 'who previously sinned and have not repented' (12.21). Additionally, there are moments of polemic and apology throughout 2 Corinthians 1–9, as others have noted as well. Horrell, for example, refers to 'the occasional digs' at

opponents in this part of the letter (1996: 310). Vegge argues that this ongoing issue, in addition to the likely presence throughout the crisis of outsiders (the 'super-apostles') willing to exploit the grievances of the minority for
its own ends, means that the language of reconciliation in 2 Corinthians 7
needs to be more carefully contextualized. Paul, he says, is actually exaggerating, or amplifying, the language of reconciliation in 2 Corinthians 7,
in ways typical of Hellenistic epideictic rhetoric, or the rhetoric of praise
and blame, in order to produce a sense of obligation on the part of the
Corinthians (Vegge 2008: 104). Paul is essentially modeling reconciliation
in such moments; indeed, he is casting the Corinthians 'as role models for
themselves' by describing, proleptically, the ideal situation of reconciliation he would like them to inhabit (Vegge 2008: 121). The same is true of
2 Corinthians 8 and 9, Vegge argues, where Paul practically reveals that
praise is a hortatory device in his rhetorical method by making plain that
his boasting about Corinth among the Macedonians will turn to shame
unless they take up the challenge of the collection (Vegge 2008: 232-34; cf.
Joubert, who calls this model an 'agonistic exemplum' [2000:173]).

There is a potential problem with the fact that Vegge's Hellenistic rhetorical sources frequently involve personal address; they deal with speeches
crafted to change the behavior of an individual. Corinth is a much more
complicated audience. Still, his careful reading of those elements in 2
Corinthians 1–9 that have been taken as evidence of redaction is rather
persuasive. The real stumbling block in Vegge's approach comes with his
discussion of 2 Corinthians 10–13. His reading of these chapters in light
of issues raised in 1 Corinthians is useful, especially insofar as its expressions of strength (e.g. 1 Cor. 4.18-21) would have contributed to the new
crisis; this draws special attention to opinions about Paul's weaknesses in
2 Cor. 10.10, particularly after the failed interim visit (Vegge 2008: 266).
Moreover, since Vegge maintains that Paul is only idealizing or modeling
reconciliation in 2 Corinthians 7, the angry tone of the final chapters
could make sense as a return to obvious and ongoing aspects of the conflict
marring his relationship with the Corinthians. Nevertheless, referring to
2 Corinthians 10–13 as 'almost a *new* tearful letter', or a text 'resembling
the tearful letter' (Vegge 2008: 36, italics original), and arguing that Paul
here is more or less duplicating the tone and style of the tearful letter in
the hopes of capitalizing on its positive effect, is tantamount to saying that
2 Corinthians 10–13 *is* the tearful letter. Despite the drawbacks, though,
when it comes to rhetorical criticism in service of theories about the unity
of 2 Corinthians, work like Vegge's seems by far the more promising, precisely because his elaboration on the rhetorical models involved so nicely
dovetails with his sharp focus on the psychological and emotional dynamics in Paul's text. It is no longer a question of formal properties, in other

words, but of modes of expression within a very specific socio-historical setting.

But unity theories need not rely on rhetorical criticism at all. James M. Scott (1998), Scott Hafemann (2000) and Frank Matera (2003) find partition theories insufficiently explanatory and overly complicated and argue for unity on grounds similar to Vegge's, namely that the tensions of 2 Corinthians 10–13 are evident elsewhere in the letter and, thus, indicate that the reconciliation of 2 Corinthians 7 is only part of the story. Paul, in 2 Corinthians 1–9, has addressed the repentant majority but, especially before he makes another visit, he must also direct his attention, in 2 Corinthians 10–13, to the minority still critical of him and his apostolic status. Murray Harris, like some partition theorists (e.g. Barrett 1973; Furnish 1984; Thrall 1994), holds that 2 Corinthians 10–13 was written later than 2 Corinthians 1–9, but only very slightly later; indeed, the entire letter would have been written over an extended period of time, according to Harris. If Paul were to have received news of a new problem, or a sudden deterioration in the Corinthian situation, he might easily have concluded the letter he had begun some months before with a sharper tone (even if one expects that Paul would probably have said something to explain the shift in tone more adequately). All of this is argued on the basis of internal evidence, though, and does not depend upon analyses of rhetorical parallels. For instance, Harris sees that the various components of 2 Corinthians concern Paul's relationship with the church and visits made, postponed or projected and this suggests a thematic unity. Moreover, the letter does have a logical organization. 'In a nutshell', Harris writes, Paul 'is saying first "I rejoice over you and have complete confidence in you" (cf. 7.4, 16), then "I urge you to finish what you have commendably begun" (cf. 8.10-11), and lastly "I am about to come, so get ready" (cf. 12.14; 13.1-11)' (2005: 52).

One of the most intriguing arguments in support of the letter's unity comes from what might appear to be an unexpected quarter. Feminist commentator Shelly Matthews (1994) agrees that rhetorical criticism offers sensible explanations of the letter's integrity, but does so for tactical reasons. Although, in general, it may be true that unity/partition theories break down along conservative/liberal lines, Matthews argues that elements of the so-called liberal view are still willing to defer to Paul's authority. A reading which claims that 2 Corinthians 10–13 precedes 2 Corinthians 1–9, as conflict precedes reconciliation, she argues, winds up promulgating a Paul who has successfully quelled dissent and stifled the voices of a critical minority. In the absence of any definitive proof to the contrary, then, she takes 2 Corinthians as a unity precisely because it allows her to suggest that the crises in Corinth, based on legitimate complaints about Paul's ministry or authentic disagreements within a burgeoning theological community, were not fully subject to Paul's control and were perhaps never resolved (cf. McCant 1988: 571-72).

2 Corinthians is a complex document, no doubt about it. Almost every transitional passage or strange shift in tone or content contributes to theories about the letter's integrity. From my perspective, despite the appeal of Vegge's and particularly Matthews' claims of formal coherence, the best explanations of 2 Corinthians require some kind of partition theory. Margaret Mitchell's is perhaps most appealing, but even simpler two-letter hypotheses do more justice to the experience of reading the epistle than any suggestions that Paul wrote 2 Corinthians in the form it has come down to us. Whether or not 2 Corinthians 10–13 should, indeed, be taken as the letter of tears must remain an open question, of course, but it is an option that I will entertain frequently in the pages that follow.

3

The Corinthian Church

We understand your message very well, though it's incomprehensible why you should be writing it to us. The splendour passes—that's what you want to persuade us of. It doesn't last. It will fade away like a starburst. It may be that *your* splendour is fading, but ours isn't. It may be that *you* need a covering to hide the fact that your face has gone dull and your figure lacklustre.

Hans Frör, *You Wretched Corinthians!*

Corinthian Critics

The title of this chapter could just as easily have been some variation of 'Paul's Opposition in Corinth'. But taking a cue from Shelly Matthews's work, and from similar efforts to recover, or re-imagine, the diverse constituencies in the communities founded and/or frequented by Paul, I am inclined to consider the individuals and groups in Corinth less tendentiously. Clearly, Paul faced opposition in Corinth, and in the next chapter we will examine his efforts at damage control. Here, though, we are interested in the Corinthian perspective(s). Of course, everything we know about the church in Corinth during the several years of its relationship with Paul comes from Paul's correspondence. Hans Frör's epistolary novel, *You Wretched Corinthians!*, is a brilliant effort at capturing in fiction the voices of the community. But the real voices of the church in 2 Corinthians are mostly lost.

1 Corinthians gives us relatively greater access to the community and its concerns. Compared to the later epistle(s) we know as 2 Corinthians, in which Paul appears only to learn about the situation in Corinth from Titus, 1 Corinthians evinces a complex communication network, with information coming to Paul by letter (7.1) and personal contacts (1.11; 11.18; 16.17-18). His mission associates and other prominent, if less-closely-allied, itinerants such as Apollos (16.12) may have brought him up to speed after their own recent visits as well. These multiple sources indicate that members of the community were choosing to affiliate themselves, perhaps on the model of the sophistic schools, with one or another Christian leader

(1.12-13; Witherington 1995: 100-101). Paul has understood from 'Chloe's people' that such affiliations signify quarreling (1.11), boasting (3.21) and judgments (4.5). Probably unrelated to this issue is the concern that members of the church are suing each other in court, 'before the unrighteous', rather than settling matters among themselves (6.1-8). The infamous case of the 'man ... living with his father's wife' (5.1) and the community's apparent lack of appreciation for the gravity of that situation, what he calls their boastful arrogance (5.2, 6), enrage Paul, inciting him to ostracize the individual (5.5, 13). Almost as significant is what Paul takes to be abuse of the community's ritual commensality, or the Lord's Supper. Because of their actions, he says, 'many of you are weak and ill, and some have died' (11.30). Finally, although Paul counts many women, including Chloe and Prisca (16.19), among his most important co-workers in this church and beyond, he appears to restrict women's religious freedom by declaring that they may not pray or prophesy 'unveiled', otherwise they risk 'disgracing [their] head[s]'—or, rather, their husbands (11.2-5). (Paul is even more restrictive at 14.33b-36, but most scholars consider this second passage an interpolation.)

If, from Paul's perspective, the Corinthians were unruly babes in the faith (3.1-4), 1 Corinthians also reveals that they were genuinely engaged correspondents, creatively active interpreters of Paul and the traditions he transmitted (see the excellent essays in Cameron and Miller 2011, which 'redescribe' the background of 1 Corinthians in terms of the social complexities of Corinthian experience). Some, including the 'arrogant' of 1 Corinthians 5, may have asserted that the gospel granted radical freedom from social strictures (cf. 7.17-18). Others, whom Paul calls 'weak' (8.11), took broadly accepted social values very seriously indeed, and refused to participate fully at events (like pagan sacrificial meals) where participation implied adherence to some of those values. Marriage and sexuality were topics of discussion, with some adhering to a regimen of chastity, while others may, self-consciously, have embraced as valuable even marriages to those outside the faith (1 Corinthians 7). Many were engaged in spiritual practices, the comparative significance of which was an open question (1 Corinthians 12). Rather than merely accepting Paul's teaching, some chose to understand resurrection (15.12) either as pertaining to Christ alone, or more simply as a metaphor, or as an opportunity for celebrating this life now (Winter 2001: 105), or perhaps as altogether misleading (Roetzel 2007: 69). Expressions, or speculative understandings, of wisdom, of one sort or another, were often key factors in several of the Corinthians' own internal discussions—although few scholars these days think this wisdom focus was Gnostic in orientation (e.g. Schmithals 1971; but see Harris who prefers the term 'proto-Gnostic' [2005: 84]).

Would many of the Corinthians themselves have characterized their interactions and attitudes, their modes of religious existence, in the ways Paul does? It seems unlikely. So unlikely that Paul's responses in 1 Corinthians to what he considers problematic behavior and theology appear 'singularly inept' to Jerome Murphy-O'Connor, for 'he makes no effort to understand their legitimate aspirations. When he is not ridiculing their intellectual pre-tensions, he simply opposes his view to theirs, without in any way trying to achieve a synthesis' (2010: 142). It is not impossible, Murphy-O'Connor suggests, that the Corinthians' anger over the tone and content of the canonical first epistle led directly to the crises behind the second (so also Horrell 1996: 218; Theissen 1994: 126; Mitchell 1991: 303). But reading the crises in 2 Corinthians for clues about what the Corinthians were up to now, further along in their relationship with Paul, is difficult. Possibly the individual mentioned in 2 Corinthians—the one who 'caused pain' (2.5) and 'did the wrong' (7.12)—is a member of the Corinthian congregation. A majority (2.6) of Corinthians punished this man for his transgression, whatever that might have been (2.1), and yet, despite this show of 'obedi-ence' (2.9), the letter goes on to suggest that the obedience of these same Corinthians is yet to be established (10.6; cf. 6.14–7.1).

What is more, Paul has evidently come under fire in Corinth for self-commendation (3.1; 10.8), for unreliability (1.17), for possible finan-cial improprieties (7.2; 11.7; 12.16-18) and for the discrepancy between his effective epistolary rhetoric and his lackluster personal performance (10.10). And to some, even his rhetoric may have been disappointing (4.3). Beyond this, however, beyond the reliance upon 'crisis' as a hermeneutic key, the paucity of information in the letter makes even speculation a challenge. To a great extent, Paul is ultimately to blame for our ignorance about the Corinthians, for he simply does not engage them transparently. Nor should we expect him to, of course. In 2 Corinthians, or the fragments that con-stitute it, Paul feels the need to defend himself against criticism while try-ing to salvage his ministry (and the collection project). His correspondents were in a much better position than we are to judge how well his apologetic and polemical remarks related to them, their prior concerns and ongoing complaints. Paul may be to blame, then, but he's not responsible. The real culprit is our (perhaps always-already Pauline) interest in determining who Paul's opponents were, especially the intruders, those 'super-apostles' (11.5; 12.11) and 'false apostles' he attacks in 2 Corinthians 10–13. While an enor-mous scholarly effort has so far failed (and will continue to fail) to identify these figures with any precision, it has frequently succeeded in relegating the Corinthians to a secondary position. For many scholars, it is a given that 1 and 2 Corinthians are different letters because the focus of 2 Corinthians is almost entirely on new problems raised, not by the Corinthians themselves, but by unwelcome interlopers. I hasten to add that this chapter will also end up playing its guilty part in granting the lion's share of its attention to the visiting itinerants.

There have been several recent scholarly caveats attempting to curb, somewhat, the tendency to read external opposition into every one of Paul's own claims (see Gooder 2006: 168; Savage 1996: 11). Here we will showcase a couple of sustained efforts at reversing the focus entirely. Jerry McCant and Margaret Mitchell, in two very different approaches to 2 Corinthians, have, nevertheless, arrived at a similar conclusion. McCant, who endorses a unity theory on rhetorical grounds, puts it bluntly: 'Perhaps it is time to close the door on discussions about opponents at Corinth' (1999: 18). The references to opponents are few and far between when compared to the number of references to Paul's feelings about, or towards, the Corinthians, he argues, and 'Paul's pastoral heart does not permit thinking of the con-gregation as "opponents"' (1999: 18). More to the point, McCant eschews 'mirror reading', that is, looking at the Pauline text as a reflection of some real situation outside of it (cf. Harris 2005: 67). This means that when 2 Corinthians appears to be discussing opponents, the most McCant feels we can adequately say is that Paul 'formulates' whatever crises and challenges the letter apparently mirrors (1999: 112). 'Pauline rhetoric, not calumnia-tors in Corinth', he claims, 'is responsible for [the] "charges"' in passages like 2 Cor. 10.10, for example (1999: 109; cf. George Lyons, who argues that 'what [Paul] says is determined by his rhetorical approach and not by his opponents' reproaches [1985: 225]). It may very well be that Pauline rhetorical formulations of opposition have something to do with Paul's *per-ception* of the situation and, accordingly, McCant will frequently refer to the way Paul 'perceived allegations of deceit' (1999: 77), for example. But, at least in theory, his approach—in some ways like that of Derridean decon-struction—does not seek answers outside the text. In practice, it is quite hard to bracket out the mirrored image. McCant sometimes does seem to focus on the Corinthian context, as when he finds an explanation for Paul's autobiographical snippet about his escape from Damascus (11.32-33) in the rivals' desire for heroic apostles (1999: 141). No one who opts out of the active search for Paul's historical opponents would deny that something was happening in Corinth, that Paul faced some sort of opposition. It is a question of finding the right ways to acknowledge this while refraining from extra-textual conclusions.

Mitchell's more recent work on the Corinthian epistles strikes this balance fairly effectively. Like McCant, she refocuses on Pauline rheto-ric as the opaque source of our information about Corinth. According to Mitchell, the letters themselves are 'the primary *agents* in the unfolding of the historical scenario (not just witnesses to it)' (2005: 322; italics original).

The crises in Corinth are crises of hermeneutical proportions, we might say, crises that arise from the Corinthian reception of Paul's rhetoric. So moments of crisis apparent in the letters are interesting to Mitchell not merely for the light they could shed on Paul's opponents, but, much more significantly, as evidence of Corinthians' reading of Paul. With respect to 2 Cor. 10.10, for example, Mitchell notes that it 'is *the first recorded moment of Pauline interpretation by someone other than Paul himself*' (Mitchell 2010: 80; italics original). And this 'someone' she regards generically as Paul's 'Corinthian critic' (2010: 13), who could just as easily be an individual as a group. Mitchell's approach seems to deal more deftly with the historical context than McCant's, although this may have more to do with the fact that Mitchell's partition theory is more compelling than McCant's assumptions about the letter's unity. Regardless, context matters for Mitchell, but rhetorically. She argues, for instance, that Paul's painful '*visit ... changed or intensified the way the Corinthians read [his] letters*' (2010: 81; italics original). That is, the visit didn't merely precipitate a crisis to which Paul responded with epistolary tears, it eventuated also in a different way of reading Paul. Some of the Corinthians, according to this view, might have been primed by the painful visit to be more acutely attentive to what Paul is doing with his language—to his style and not just his content. If they were now suspicious of his motives, they might find further justification for their concerns in his own rhetorical performances. Outside opponents may or may not have been an issue, for Mitchell, because what matters most, and what is most available to us now, is how Paul and his community interpreted each other. The general validity of such an approach increases when studies of specific verses similarly suggest a complex hermeneutical situation, as in Hans Dieter Betz's examination of 'the inner man' of 2 Cor. 4.16. Betz argues that Paul's idea may well have a Platonic background, but it is much more likely to have developed in the 'dialogical context' in which Paul and his collaborators engaged with the vocabulary and ideas of the Corinthians. Reading the verse this way 'it is impossible to say who came up with the idea [of the inner man] first' (Betz 2000: 320).

Beyond the salutary awareness of the dynamic role they continued to play as recipients of Paul's letters, what can an approach that privileges the Corinthians themselves tell us? In general, we can say that the Corinthians, in one way or another, were to some extent critical in their assessment of Paul's apostolic authority. One area of research supporting this view comes, again, out of rhetorical studies and focuses on the fact that the interpretation of Paul preserved in 2 Cor. 10.10 seems to indicate sensitivity to rhetorical self-presentation. Public rhetorical jousts were 'ubiquitous', as Dale Martin has noted, and both Paul and the Corinthians would have witnessed, or heard, professional rhetors in any number of ordinary urban contexts (Martin 1999: 49-51). The criticism of Paul in 2 Cor. 10.10 sounds like criticism of the unlettered on the part of those who had received rhetorical training (especially among the elite). Those with rhetorical skill were expected to be, analogously, beautiful in body and status. Paul's weaknesses and possible illnesses, not to mention his uncertain status (he is not, after all, a 'super apostle'), may have suggested that there is something fraudulent going on in his letter writing: how is it possible at all for his letters to be weighty when, physically at any rate, Paul is not recognizable as a rhetor? Paul might retort that he does, indeed, have some rhetorical training, even if he is not a professional. Martin reads 2 Cor. 11.6 as 'layman with regard to speech', rather than, as in the NRSV, 'untrained in speech' (1999: 48). But, to Greco-Roman audiences, Paul's bodily weaknesses, his proneness to suffering, would still have proven a challenge to their understanding of his rhetoric and may even have indicated potential defects in his character (Martin 1999: 55; cf. Glancy 2010: 44). Paul's physical traumas, his beatings especially (2 Cor. 11.24; cf. 1.9), might have signaled, as well, a culturally coded effeminacy that, as Jennifer Larson argues, would have rendered some of his behavior more legible as feminine (his vacillation with regard to whether or not to visit Corinth, for instance) and, hence, less obviously worthy of the Corinthians' respect (Larson 2004: 92-93, drawing upon Marshall 1987). Certainly, the Corinthians had apparently begun to have serious doubts that Christ spoke in Paul. As scholars have rightly noted, the criticism in 2 Cor. 13.3 is clearly from the Corinthians themselves, although what they were demanding of Paul and whether or not it concerned matters of discipline, is debated (see the summary of perspectives in Thrall 2000: 878-82).

Paul's financial planning is another area of scholarly focus. It seems obvious that money issues somehow plagued his Corinthian ministry and that these pertained to the collection, on the one hand (7.2; 8.20; 12.17-18) and, possibly, to the Hellenistic system of patronage, on the other (11.7-11). 2 Corinthians 12.16 is perhaps the vital hinge for understanding both of these issues. Here, Paul avers, again, that he 'did not burden' the Corinthians by accepting payment from them for his ministry. 'Nevertheless,' he goes on, 'since I was crafty [according to his critics], I took you in by deceit.' Most commentators understand this verse to mean that Paul was accused of embezzling from, or otherwise taking some personal advantage of, the collection in order to support himself, while ostentatiously refusing the direct assistance the community had offered to him. It could also be that the Corinthians felt that Paul had deceived them about his financial independence (Martin 1999: 84). After all, in 1 Corinthians 9, he acknowledges the right of apostles to be supported by those evangelized, but declares boldly that he 'would rather die' than accept their money, since preaching 'the gospel free of charge' is one of his proudest boasts (1 Cor. 9.18; 2 Cor. 11.10). And yet, in our text, he acknowledges, petulantly, what the Corinthians may have discovered on their own, that in fact he did accept money for his work from other churches (11.8-9; cf. Phil. 4.15-18). This may or may not amount to deception (see Long's criticism of Martin on this topic in Long 2004: 130), and many commentators believe that Paul probably stuck to a simple policy of taking money only from communities where he was not currently resident. One can also understand the 'double blessing' of 2 Cor. 1.15 to refer to the benefit the Corinthians will gain from giving Paul material aid (so Fee 2001: 102). If so, the fact that Paul now intends to allow the Corinthians to do him this service even though he had previously, when living with them, adamantly refused their offers of assistance, might have led to the conflict with the offending individual of 1.5 and 7.12 (see Downs 2008: 46-47).

In any event, the Corinthians seem to have had trouble understanding precisely what Paul was up to. And not only the Corinthians. The delegates mentioned in 8.18-23 and 9.3 were 'appointed' and sent quite possibly by the Macedonian churches (and/or those of Asia, according to Thrall 2000: 549). If it is true that Paul leaves them unnamed because he wanted to avoid 'giving them more status than [he thought] was due', as Betz suggests (1985: 73), this may reflect some concern with Paul's management of the collection on the part of other communities involved. Nevertheless, most readers assume that Paul was probably involved in creating this delegation. In Matera's view, the quasi-independence of individuals appointed by other churches would, additionally, have been helpful as a validation of Paul's probity (2003: 197).

Did Paul's financial independence mean, in the logic of 1 Corinthians 9, that Paul himself didn't have the right to claim the title of apostle (Murphy-O'Connor 2010: 46; see Downs's reconstruction of the opponents' criticism in this regard in 2008: 52)? Or did it imply Paul's 'unwillingness to enter into a relationship of mutuality' with the Corinthian church (Matthews 1993: 211)? Why did he refuse their 'gesture of love' (Murphy-O'Connor 1996: 305)? Did he think them inferior to other churches with whom he had evidently established some form of reciprocity similar to the kind they were offering (Thrall 2000: 704)? Much attention in New Testament scholarship has been focused on the ancient patronage system. In general terms, the receipt of gifts could signal an imbalance in social status, and the patron-client relationships that developed could tend towards exploitation. Perhaps some group among the Corinthians was hoping, by means of a gift, to claim certain rights to Paul's ministry. Commentators tend to take Paul's own attestations of subordination (2 Cor. 4.5; c.f. 1.6; 12.15) seriously, and most read the refusal of lordship at 1.24 as an important limit concept; Christians can be servants or slaves of one another but not masters. But do we really know how this language played in Corinth? If Paul were already committing himself in service to the Corinthians, could not they have assumed that their reciprocal service to him would likewise be welcome and that any donations made to other Christian itinerants would be viewed similarly—and not as a purely mercantile purchasing of influence (2.17)? Or, more critically, might they not have been concerned to balance the scales of obligation with a gift to Paul in response to his generosity toward them? Such a possibility 'should not be sublimated by theological rationales' (Cameron and Miller 2011: 291). Paul is frequently assumed to be shunning patronage in order to maintain his freedom. Why could the Corinthians not be similarly motivated, especially if Paul himself were 'seek[ing] to establish and maintain a relationship of [patron-client] dependency on the grounds of his preaching of the gospel' (p. 291)?

One rather engagingly idiosyncratic reading takes part of Paul's financial quandary in an entirely different direction. Margaret Thrall posits that Paul, during his intermediate visit, was given a sum of cash by an individual for the collection. Soon thereafter the money was stolen, and, although Paul could guess the identity of the thief, he couldn't prove the man's guilt. Since, for whatever reason, the Corinthians didn't entirely believe Paul, he could make no headway in recovering the stolen money, and he departed under a cloud. His letter of tears then shamed the Corinthians into carrying out a 'further investigation, which resulted in the offender's confession and punishment', as well as the rest of the community's repentance (1994: 68).

Obstreperous Outsiders

Mitchell's (and McCant's) insight, that Pauline rhetoric and its reception in Corinth are the principle factors motivating the crises of this epistle, helps us to construct, imaginatively, a fuller context for the Corinthians in their debates with, or criticism of, Paul. As mentioned above, however, scholarly interest is predominantly focused on Paul's opponents—as though the Corinthians themselves were merely a field of battle across which our heroic apostle strides. So, to paraphrase everyone who has ever paraphrased Raymond Carver, what are we talking about when we talk about the opponents?

For starters, it is usually assumed that some Corinthians were supporters of the intruder-missionaries with whom Paul was in conflict. The starkness of my suggestion, above, that the scholarship ignores the church in favor of studies of the Pauline opposition, thus needs to be modified, but only slightly, for few actually credit the Corinthians with much more than the vague notion of support. Perhaps this support was even limited to an individual host, the very person Paul singles out in 2.5 and 7.12

(Horrell 1996: 222; Barrett 1973: 291). Some believe that there might have been diverse pockets of discontent (Barnett 1997: 453) or perhaps even a 'critical minority' whose interests were exploited by the visiting opposition (Vegge 2008: 270). Jerome Murphy-O'Connor gives this last idea a great deal of traction by detailing the possibility of coordination between the outside opponents and a group of Corinthian Spirit-people ('those who are spiritual', 1 Cor. 2.15 NRSV). The Spirit-people were, or considered themselves to be, acolytes of Apollos, in Murphy-O'Connor's reading. They felt that their wisdom entailed their perfection (1 Cor. 2.6) and that, 'as possessors of "the Spirit which is from God" (2.12)', they were '"filled (with divine blessings)", "wealthy", "kings" (4.8), "wise", "strong", [and] "honoured" (4.10)' (1996: 280). Apollos imparted to the Spirit-people a 'Philonic perspective', especially with regard to Moses, who for Philo epitomized 'Hellenistic virtues' (Murphy-O'Connor 1991: 34-35). In canonical 1 Corinthians, Paul offended this group in particular by mocking their pretensions and undermining their wisdom claims. By the time he writes 2 Corinthians, however, he realizes that he must find a way to appease this constituency, or risk losing them entirely. So, he 'appropriat[es] two key words from their lexicon, namely "spirit" and "freedom"', and deploys them in his treatment of Moses in 2 Corinthians 3 in an effort to win them back to his cause (Murphy-O'Connor 1991: 37).

Murphy-O'Connor's portrait of the Spirit-people is not at all unique or very controversial (*pace* Meyer 2009: 107), even if their connection with Apollos must remain purely speculative. Less comprehensible is the pact he imagines them to have formed with the visiting opponents, whom he considers 'Judaizers' from Antioch intent on spreading a Torah-based gospel in Pauline communities. It may be true, as Murphy-O'Connor indicates, that odd political alliances are formed all the time in order to defeat a common enemy, but it is difficult to imagine the two groups as he describes them ('free-thinking Hellenistic pseudo-philosophic believers' on the one hand, and 'Law-observant Jewish Christians' on the other) undertaking the compromises necessary to join forces against Paul (Murphy-O'Connor 1996: 303; Harris refers to an analogous uneasy coalition between 'proto-Gnostics' and Judaizers [2005: 86-87]).

Nevertheless, that the opponents are 'Judaizers' is a notion with a long history, stretching in modern scholarship from F.C. Baur (1875) to the most recent commentaries. Paul, in 2 Corinthians 11, seems to acknowledge that his opponents, who have come from elsewhere (11.4), identify themselves as Hebrews, Israelites, descendants of Abraham (11.22), as well as 'ministers of Christ' (11.23). Of course, Paul can match them on these grounds, point by point, and he does so, upping the ante by declaring: 'I am a better one' (11.23). But, if what Paul says really does mirror the claims and activities of the rival ministers, they would seem to be 'Judaizers' of a different sort from those who are 'bewitching' the Galatians by promoting circumcision among Gentile adherents to Paul's gospel (Gal. 3.1; cf. Phil. 3.2-6). Like those opponents, the Corinthian rivals are, polemically, accused of 'proclaim[ing] another Jesus' and 'a different gospel', of communicating 'a different spirit' (2 Cor. 11.4; Gal. 1.6-9). But nowhere in 2 Corinthians is circumcision even mentioned, nor is anything approaching Paul's clash with Peter in Antioch over Jewish–Gentile table fellowship (Gal. 2.11-14). Instead, the conflicts here revolve around: the quality of the rivals' rhetorical self-presentation (10.10; 11.6; cf. 10.12); their ability as ecstatics to perform 'signs and wonders' (12.1-12; cf. 5.12-13); their pedigree (3.1; 11.22); their understanding of the mission field (10.13-15); and their receptiveness to Corinthian benefactors (11.7-9, 19; 12.13). These differences have led many to abandon the term 'Judaizer' altogether.

We will explore what this identification implies in a moment. First it is important to point out that the term 'Judaizer' is usually dropped merely for methodological purposes—as in Furnish's commentary, which agrees, on evidentiary grounds, that Paul was dealing with 'Judaizers' in Galatians, but not in 2 Corinthians (1984: 53). But there are also compelling ideological reasons for leaving 'Judaizer' behind. Mark Nanos reminds us that the term has 'historically been used as if there is something self-evidently wrong with Jews ... who might seek to persuade non-Jews to become proselytes' (2011: 1; cf. Sumney 2005: 49-50). Recent New Testament scholarship, sensitive to this and other problems, has begun to be much more careful in discussing ancient Jews as they appear in Christian texts, sometimes preferring the transliteration *Ioudaioi* 'to signal the complexity and variety of such ethnic descriptive terms' as 'Jews or Judeans' (Marchal 2009: 110). To understand the need for greater sensitivity, one only has to look at how easily 'Judaizer' sets Jewishness in stark opposition to Pauline Christianity. In Murray Harris's commentary, for instance, 'Judaizers' are, in fact, *not* Christians, but rather Jews who, while 'claiming to be Christian', actually 'try to impose Jewish practices upon Gentiles' and, presumably, because of this difference, they manifest a 'virulent antipathy' to Paul's Christian (read: universal or free, i.e. not imposed) gospel (2005: 85-86). Obviously, given the fact that the rivals' status as ministers of Christ (11.23) is not challenged by Paul, they are Christian (too), just as Paul is Jewish (too). Undoubtedly, Harris is motivated in his assessment by a kind of prejudice, but a prejudice directed against Paul's opposition in general; he can characterize some of the Gentile Corinthians' own alleged misinterpretations of Paul as 'malicious' (2005: 81), for instance, simply because they are misinterpretations of a distinctly non-Pauline theological stamp. That is, it is not always a question of intentional anti-Judaism. But such readings can, nevertheless, participate, even unwittingly, in a broader, more specifically bigoted, cultural history.

Rather than continuing with 'Judaizers', then, we might refer to the rival missionaries as 'Hellenistic-Jewish Christians' (e.g. Furnish 1984: 534), or 'itinerant apostles' who were 'Hellenistic Jews of the Diaspora' (Roetzel 2007: 37, 108), or 'Greek-speaking Jews ... from Judea who also recognized Jesus to be the Christ' (Barnett 1997: 35; see the useful list indicating the range of interpretations in Harris 2005: 79-80). The only problem with such designations is that they are also applicable, more or less, to Paul. Frequently such similarities are lost on the commentators. Thus, Paul Barnett implies, for example, that the Jewish fascination with signs is already something Paul criticized in 1 Cor. 1.22 (1997: 35), but that Paul's authenticity as an apostle was manifested by his working divinely-inspired signs, which the false apostles were somehow incapable of producing (1997: 580)—even though earlier the rivals were said, paradoxically, to be given to 'apocalyptic fervor expressed in prophetic inspiration and miraculous signs' (1997: 35). Alan Segal's intriguing reading of the opponents as people insisting upon certain (developing) Jewish customs both allows for a connection with Jewish-Christian practice and more clearly distinguishes the opponents from Paul. Paul mentions Moses' veil in 2 Cor. 3.15-18, according to Segal, not only because of its metaphorical significance, but also because his opponents, and perhaps the community as a whole, may have been ritually veiling themselves with prayer shawls in order to be reverential and, possibly, to achieve mystical states (1990: 153). Segal still relies to some extent upon the concept of the 'Judaizer' (with regard to Galatians particularly), but by focusing here on a ritual practice of indeterminate origin, embraced by unidentifiable, perhaps even non-Jewish opponents, he nicely foregrounds the complexity of lived identity questions in the early church (see also Lincoln for a similarly open-ended look at the plurality of positions behind the otherwise monolithic concept of the 'Judaizer' [1981: 56]).

Among several additional issues raised in discussions of Paul's opponents, it is often noted that Paul refers to them in two different ways, as false apostles (11.13) and as super-apostles (11.5; 12.11). A great many readers over the centuries have argued that these are in fact two different groups: the rival itinerants, on the one hand, and the Jerusalem apostles, on the other. This is because Paul himself seems to treat the two titles differently. The false apostles are minions of Satan, disguised as 'apostles of Christ' (11.13-15). As far as the super-apostles are concerned, Paul may merely say that he is 'not in the least inferior to them' (11.5; 12.11). It is simply inconceivable to some that Paul would claim more or less equal status with satanic imposters (e.g. Harris 2005: 746-47; see the useful survey of such readings in Thrall 2000: 676). Most scholars, even those who think the super-apostles are probably Peter, James and John, can hear irony in Paul's appellation for them—something akin to Paul's snide praise for the Jerusalem 'pillars' in Gal. 2.9 (Barrett 1973: 278). Contemporary scholarship has, by and large, taken another approach to the matter, and most interpreters now think that Paul is alluding to only the one group of visiting rivals. This reading makes the most sense of a number of factors, including the following. The transition between 11.4 and 11.5 is more fluid if the 'someone who comes' and the 'super-apostles' are one and the same, especially as a version of the same criticism recurs again in 11.12-13, with unambiguous reference to the rivals on the scene. Paul Barnett has noted that *hyper*-words frequently appear in this section (10.14, 16; 12.7), and in critical contrast with the so-called false apostles, which would imply that the super in the title *super*-apostles [*hyperlian apostolōn*] involves a similarly targeted gibe (1997: 523; cf. Mitchell who prefers the appropriately silly 'super-duper apostles' [2010: 82]).

The opponents also appear to have brought with them to Corinth letters of recommendation, and they hope to leave with recommendations from the Corinthians. Paul, in 2 Cor. 3.1, asks: 'surely we do not need, as some do, letters of recommendation to you or from you, do we?' While scholars have argued that the letters might have come from Jerusalem, most now agree that they were in all likelihood testimonials and/or requests for basic assistance of the kind that Paul himself wrote (e.g. 2 Cor. 8.23-24; Rom. 16.1-2). The letters themselves were, thus, not at issue, but rather the fact that Paul neither carried such letters himself, nor asked the Corinthians for their recommendation. Interestingly, despite the very general awareness that letters of recommendation like these were extremely common in Paul's day, scholars still want to link them to one or another 'official' or 'authority' in the early church. If 10.13-18 refers to the agreement mentioned in Gal. 2.9 (*pace* Matera 2003: 231-33 and Furnish 1983: 481, although I think they are correct that it does not), then authorities and official concordats and the like must, indeed, be a factor. Certainly, it is possible that the Antiochene church (so Murphy-O'Connor), or perhaps Peter (so Thrall), was trying to reassert centralized control over Paul's far-flung, untethered ministry. In his recollection of the conflict with Peter in Antioch in Galatians, Paul clearly evinces an awareness of the significance of the mother church. And the collection he hopes to bring to Jerusalem has very frequently been considered, at least in part, a political maneuver, the aim of which is to secure implicit official recognition from the pillars of the church.

But, in addition to Paul's own recommendation-free operation, the New Testament tells of other independent agents, such as the exorcist who uses Jesus' name without authorization (Mk 9.38-41; Lk. 9.49-50) and the passage in Acts 8 about Simon Magus. Even if Acts 15.24-25 strongly implies that Jerusalem tried to crack down on dissident, unauthorized itinerants by delegating official representatives, that does not clarify our understanding of the situation in Corinth—the opponents were asking for letters *from* the Corinthians. Although Peter and Apollos are both mentioned in 1 Corinthians, no similar 'authorities' are mentioned by Paul in 2 Corinthians, as one would expect were they behind the newcomers. Even if 'officials' from Jerusalem were somehow involved, the situation might have looked rather different to them than to those who sympathized with Paul's plight. According to Margaret Thrall, 'From the angle of vision of the authorities in Jerusalem, it would look as though Paul is creating an independent ecclesiastical empire ... Paul would have been seen as wanting to have it both ways. On the one hand, he insisted that Gentile Christians were as much a part of the people of God as Jewish Christians. But, on the other hand, he wanted to keep control of these groups himself' (2000: 954). This would be the case especially if Gal. 2.9 did not refer to geographically exclusive zones of activity, or if Paul's account of the agreement masks a real uncertainty about its terms (as in Boer 2011: 127; Segal 1990: 189-91). After all, it is not impossible that even Peter, or a party associated with his name, may have been welcome in Corinth early on, despite the fact that Corinth 'belonged' to Paul (Barrett 2004: 83; cf. Fitzmyer 2008: 143-45).

Georgian Revival?

One of the most influential interpretations of Paul's rivals in the last half century is Dieter Georgi's study, *The Opponents of Paul in Second Corinthians*, originally published in 1964. Indeed, his work arguably informs the conclusions of all the scholars mentioned in the previous paragraph. Georgi proposed that Paul's opponents combined elements of Jewish missionary practice, scriptural interpretation akin to that of Jewish apologists (such as Josephus and Philo), and pagan religious speculation, especially in their treatment of major figures in the tradition as 'divine men'. Georgi's idea of 'the [divine man/*theios anēr*] motif' (1986: 155) helps to make sense of Paul's focus on Moses in 2 Corinthians 3. Moses would have been venerated as a glorious individual in whom the divine was present. Divine men participate in God's creative power, and in their ability to work mighty deeds 'they embody the universe and its order' (1986: 133). The opponents are likely to have come to Corinth with a special interest in promoting Christ as a divine man like Moses. But they and their adherents could also draw near the divine in their exegesis, for scripture is 'an archive of the spirit' in their view, and interpretation brings immediacy to this pneumatic source, allows them to 'heighten vital consciousness beyond human limits'—indeed, to have, via textual exposition, mystical experiences (1986: 147).

Scholars have been critical of Georgi's work. Many have alleged that there is little historical evidence for the kind of Jewish missionary outreach to Gentiles upon which Georgi builds much of his case (Paget 2010: 157; Ware 2005: 54-55; Thrall 2000: 936; but see Rudolph who claims that perhaps Georgi's 'maximalist' view merely exaggerates the extent of the phenomenon [2011: 136]). Another complaint is that 'divine men' would not need letters of recommendation, for their deeds should speak for themselves (Murphy-O'Connor 2010: 30; Savage 1996: 9). Some scholars doubt whether or not Georgi's 'divine man' motif can actually be considered viable historically (Holladay 1977; Blackburn 1991: 70). Perhaps more serious is the fact that Paul's apparent critique of his opponents' position on Moses actually endorses some of the claims one expects the opponents to be making. In other words, God's glory can be experienced in Moses and Jesus, especially for those, like Georgi's missionaries, who are adept at exegesis. It is true that Paul seems to denigrate Moses—his ministry is the ministry of death (3.7) and condemnation (3.9), and it is also perhaps something of a deception (3.13). Yet, as Scott Hafemann points out, Paul's comparison of Moses' glory with that of the spirit available with Christ does not suggest an ontological difference. The glory of the latter is not better. It is the *same* glory. Paul believes that his gospel offers unmediated access to it, when compared to Moses' veil, but a strong continuity remains (Hafemann 1996: 271), as would be the case for the opponents in Georgi's reading (1986: 271). Moreover, it could be that Paul actually takes Moses' ministry of death for granted. That is, he does not argue the point, but merely asserts it, as if this were an assumption shared by his audience as well (Thrall 1994: 240, 246-48). If this is true, then he seems not to have been worried that his rivals were promoting Moses in the way Georgi proposes they were.

Nevertheless, many continue to develop Georgi's insights (e.g. Roetzel 2007: 36-37; Larson 2004: 96-97; Witherington 1995: 383; cf. Matthews 2001; Bormann *et al.* 1994). One that I think requires additional emphasis is that the Hellenistic religious context was a neutral zone of competing ideas and strategies. According to Georgi, 'the opponents saw the essence of proclamation in competition' (1986: 236). But he finds the same paradigm at work in the New Testament. He considers the competition between Philip and Simon in Acts 8 to be precisely analogous to competing pneumatic missionaries from 'different denominations': '[I]t cannot be said'—as, in fact, it is often said of Paul's opponents (e.g. by Hafemann 2000: 412)—'that one only demonstrates his personality, the other, in contrast, the authority standing behind him. Both do both!' (1986: 169). The same must be true for Paul as well as the rival missionaries in Corinth (*pace* Georgi himself, who holds that Paul did *not* compete [1986: 236; 2005: 114]). The project of adapting this dimension of his work has merit, and echoes are to be found in readings like that of Margaret Thrall, according to which Paul's miracle-working opponents did, indeed, force him into competition for adherents in Corinth (2000: 841, 938; see, also, the essays in Cameron and Miller 2011). In the next chapter we will discuss a few readings that take things a step further by turning the tables and holding Paul accountable for his own unnecessarily 'virulent' attacks upon rival missionaries who, in the end, could be said merely to 'exercise their ministries differently' (Matera 2003: 24).

4

Damage Control

If I didn't know how sincere, how true you are, I would say you were a ruthless politician.

—Donn-Byrne, *Brother Saul*

The Personal may be Political

2 Corinthians is often called the most personal of Paul's letters both because Paul's responses to many of the criticisms mentioned in the last chapter involve extensive autobiographical detail and also because of the letter's emotional range—from tenderness to biting sarcasm. The turn to rhetorical research has formally contextualized Paul's personal expressions, but rarely has the study of his carefully crafted emotional appeals, for instance, led to a critical rhetorical reception of his sincerity. Fredrick Long concludes his reading of the letter by asserting that it 'is Paul's great apology, in which he opens wide his heart and wants the Corinthians to do the same', taking the language of 2 Cor. 6.11-13 as unmediated by over-arching persuasive aims (2004: 230). Undoubtedly, one can be sincere while self-consciously adapting rhetorical forms, and even the most sincere of expressions necessarily draws upon literary/rhetorical conventions. Paul's sincerity can probably be measured on a sliding scale that may not have as its terminal points the opposition between truth and cynical manipulation—or 'ruthless politics' in the words of Irish novelist Donn-Byrne's Barnabas. Such obvious binaries are likely to be less than helpful. Nevertheless, scholarly inquiry into Paul's own self-defense and self-presentation needs to allow for a critical distance between the epistolary context and Paul's statements about it, even in the most personal of Pauline letters. For, as George Lyons argues with regard to autobiographical content in Galatians and 1 Thessalonians, 'Paul's rhetorical motives suggest that ethical characterization and edification were of greater concern than historical completeness and exactitude'. That is, even when he seems to be talking about himself, Paul may really be constructing models (on the basis of scriptures, tradition, the gospel, etc., rather than simply first-hand experience) in the hopes of shaping his

audience's response (1985: 226). And, to some extent, efforts of this sort may be easier to spot in 2 Corinthians simply because the scope that Paul grants to his own self-commentary brings his mimetic parallels (to Christ's suffering, for instance) more clearly to our attention. It will be important, whenever possible, to reflect critically upon Paul's rhetorically astute auto-biographical and apostolic presence in the letter as part of our continuing effort to challenge the normative ways in which Paul is most often read. More often than not, commentators will devote considerable attention to Paul's defense of his apostolic status. There is no doubt that 2 Corinthians reveals serious early questions about who qualifies as an apostle and why, and about who gets to make that call. In Paul's mind, at least, there are 'signs' that, when performed, validate one's 'true' apostolic identity (12.12). But, given the very real possibility that conflict and polemic—if not a more basic interest in constructing his own power (Schütz 1975: 204)—are significantly responsible for the parameters of apostolic authority as outlined by Paul, it would be a mistake to privilege his perspective on the topic.

We have already discussed some of the more Corinth-specific personal data above, including Paul's planned and intermediate visits (1.15-17, 23; 2.1; 13.1), his difficulty in Corinth with an offending individual (2.5; 7.12), his tearful letter (2.4; 7.8), his narrative of anxious waiting for word from Titus (2.12-13; 7.6), his handling of financial matters (7.2; 12.13-18) and, in 2 Corinthians 10–13 (cf. 2.17; 3.1), his earlier and/or later troubles with rival missionaries. Additionally, Paul talks about his tendency to boast too much (10.8), his authority both to forgive and punish (2.10; 10.6; 13.2) and his previous and future fund-raising activities among the churches (8–9). We will address these last details in later sections of this chapter.

In terms of the broader context behind 2 Corinthians, Paul more than hints at some dire, life-threatening circumstance 'in Asia' which he survived only with the help of God. Things were so terrible for him that it was as though he did die, in fact, and was raised from the dead (1.8-10). N.T. Wright, drawing attention to Paul's Pharisaic heritage (which featured a belief in resurrection) as well as to various scriptural resources (e.g. Ps. 16.10) upon which Paul may have relied, characterizes the notion here as 'inaugurated eschatology in the service of urgent pastoral need' (2003: 301). His divinely accomplished rescue is part and parcel of the coming resurrection, even in the present. No one can say just what caused Paul to feel 'so utterly, unbearably crushed' (1.8), but many have imagined, however improbably, that it took place in Ephesus at the time of the riot in Acts 19 (which is not described as a threat to Paul), or the struggle with wild animals mentioned in 1 Cor. 15.32 (which most take as metaphorical). Was it an imprisonment—even the imprisonment of Phil. 1.12-30 (so Furnish 1984: 123)—under judicial death sentence? A violent attack?

A near-mortal illness? Or perhaps it was the sting of regret after he had written the letter of tears? David Fredrickson entertains this last idea in his discussion of Paul's strategy of rhetorically exaggerating his suffering in accordance with Hellenistic conventions of friendship, reconciliation and moral exhortation. Paul caused the Corinthians suffering with his letter, but he did so only in order to aid them (2 Cor. 7.9). Now that he knows their response, he plays up his own suffering to show that he shares with them in their pain (see 2 Cor. 1.3-7), as is expected of a true friend (Fredrickson 2003: 181). The courage required to face such suffering, however, exemplified in particular by Paul's hardship lists in 2 Cor. 4.8-12 and 6.3-10, is meant to remind his readers that he *is* still serious and can make good on his threats (e.g. 2 Cor. 10.6; 2003: 185). Proposals that Paul's suffering arises from his emotional turmoil vis-à-vis the Corinthians are not entirely compelling (see Thrall 1994: 115), but Fredrickson's idea is still valuable in that it allows for a greater degree of self-consciousness on Paul's part than is common, despite the fact that such self-consciousness is usually implied. For example, Barrett thinks both that 2 Cor. 1.8 refers to a real situation, an unexpected horror that shaped Paul's subsequent outlook (cf. Dodd who calls the transformation Paul's 'second conversion' [1967: 81]) *and* that it is thematically relevant for the problems he faces in Corinth (1973: 66; cf. Furnish 1984: 124). Whatever the trial Paul suffered in Asia, it seems more reasonable to suggest that he makes very shrewd use of it here, rather than to imply a merely serendipitous pastoral relevance to Paul's brief anecdote.

In some of the more tantalizing passages in 2 Corinthians, Paul writes of his own more distant past. He says that 'we once knew Christ from a human point of view' and that 'we know him no longer in that way' (5.16). While a few might allow for an actual historical connection with Jesus (so, e.g., Barnett 1997: 295), most scholars take *kata sarka* adverbially, 'we knew ... from a human point of view', and so understand Paul simply to be underscoring his refusal to judge anyone by merely worldly or, more specifically, unspiritual standards.

In another hardship list, Paul enumerates what may be actual experiences: imprisonments, lashings at the hands of Jews, floggings by Roman authorities, a stoning, shipwrecks, dangerous journeys and so on (11.23-29). Each element in this list has attracted extensive commentary, but none can be adequately correlated with equivalent episodes in Acts, for, even when similar circumstances are mentioned, either the chronology fails to cohere (e.g. the shipwreck in Acts 27 takes place only at the end of Paul's career) or the suggested numbers seem improbably off (e.g. compare 'far more imprisonments' to the one incarceration, up to this point, in Acts 16). Paul's own letters are scarcely more helpful, since it is uncertain whether the imprisonments of Philippians and Philemon are individual or separate incidents and whether they are earlier or later than 2 Corinthians—although most scholars, trying to link them with Paul's imprisonments at the end of Acts, would say later. The traditional thirty-nine lashes (11.24) might have been received for undermining Torah observance among some (i.e. the God-fearers?) in the synagogues or for any number of other reasons (Harris 2005: 802). The beatings with rods, a Roman punishment, could call into question Paul's citizenship, which is alleged by Luke in conjunction with a Roman flogging (Acts 16.37). Many of the other hardships listed here seem quite generic, the kind of troubles anyone, like Paul, traveling extensively on foot or at sea, would encounter. More pertinent perhaps than the issue of historical accuracy, then, is the significance of the list as a whole. Most readers take Paul seriously, but some, nevertheless, also detect a certain parodic tone, especially in Paul's use of enumeration ('five times', 'three times', 'once', etc.), which mirrors lists of the accomplishments of leaders like Alexander or Augustus (Furnish 1984: 515; cf. Welborn 1999: 143)—the thrill of heroic victory transposed into the agony of apostolic defeat. Paul prefaces this list with what might be a caveat: he is going to boast now as a fool and a madman (11.21, 23). That he then goes on to brag about what could be considered his shameful escape from Damascus (11.32-33) only heightens the sense that, even if Paul has real experiences in mind, he is framing them ironically (in this case as an inversion of military heroics; Judge 2008: 706-708; cf. Glancy 2004), the better to make his opponents, boasters in earnest, look like fools. This would be all the more effective if a contingent, perhaps a majority, of the Corinthians tended to agree, with Paul, that Christ is better represented in weakness (12.8-10; 13.4) than in glory.

This parody of excessive boastfulness intensifies in the final major auto-biographical detail we shall discuss, the heavenly journey of 12.1-10. In this passage, Paul writes about an ecstatic, visionary ascent that he (or an anonymous 'person in Christ') experienced 'fourteen years ago' (12.2). While Acts understands Paul to have been subject to frequent visions and auditions (16.9; 18.9-11; 22.17-21) as well as the three conversion reports (9.1-19; 22.6-11; 26.12-18)—not to mention miracles (e.g. 19.11-12)—the epistles are much more reticent witnesses of Paul's mystical experiences (1 Cor. 9.1; 15.8; Gal. 1.12, 16; 2.2). Certainly, he refers to the gifts of the spirit (e.g. 1 Cor. 14.18), and his apocalypticism (e.g. 1 Thess. 4.15–5.11) may have had some ecstatic input, but the passage in 2 Corinthians 12 is without parallel in the Pauline corpus. It should come as no surprise that readers have imagined Paul to be speaking of his own conversion here, given the uniqueness of the passage. If other passages—for example: the imagery of light shining out of darkness in 4.6 (Hubbard 2004: 158; Theissen 1987: 123); the language of turning in 3.16 (Kim 2001: 179); Paul's many references to suffering (Segal 1990: 68)—recollect elements of Paul's Christophany as well, then it would seem that 2 Corinthians, as a whole, is an essential document for reconstructions of Paul's earliest Christian moments. The majority of scholars agree, however, that 2 Corinthians 12 probably does not refer to the Damascus event narrated by Acts, since Luke writes of light and a voice experienced on an earthly road, whereas Paul is recounting a heavenly journey. What is more, the chronology simply does not work. If 2 Corinthians was written about 56 CE, then Paul's 'fourteen years ago' would have fallen in 42 CE, years too late for any correspondence between text and event (but see Segal who grants the remote possibility that the passage describes Paul's conversion [1990: 36-37]; cf. Morray-Jones who finds a connection with the different moment of Acts 22.17-21 [1993: 286]).

Still, it is generally taken for granted that Paul is here speaking of himself, despite his use of the third person. There have been various proposals for understanding this visionary journey—or, journeys, if one takes 'to the third heaven' (12.2) and 'into Paradise' (12.4) to refer to two separate incidents (Ashton 2000: 119). Many scholars are now comfortable referring to Paul's mystical experiences and many discuss such experiences, in the context of Jewish mystical, visionary and/or apocalyptic texts of the sort with which Paul would have been familiar. Andrew Lincoln's excellent survey of such wildly divergent literary parallels may raise more questions than can be answered about the architecture of the Pauline cosmos, but it clearly situates Paul within perspectives that associated the third heaven with Paradise, that imagined bodily journeys into the spiritual realm (2 Cor. 12.2-3), and that insisted upon the secrecy of the messages imparted there (12.4). Even the 'thorn in the flesh', which Paul said he received 'to keep [him] from being too elated' by his mystical journey (12.7), seems to have a parallel in rabbinic literature (Lincoln 1981: 77-85; but see Gooder who notes significant discrepancies between Paul and the sources Lincoln, and others, cite [2006]). Paul does not clearly claim this experience as his own, referring to an unknown 'man' instead, but that may also have its roots in convention, especially if rabbinic rules disallowing 'public discussion of mystic phenomena' predate Paul (Segal 1990: 58). Or perhaps it could be that Paul is referring not generally to himself, but specifically to his 'heavenly self', his person transformed into an 'angelic ... likeness' (Morray-Jones 1993: 273). Readers a tad wary of the mystical in Pauline scholarship will sometimes argue that Paul shies away from using the first person out of humility. The opponents have painted him into a corner and so he must fight fire with fire by bringing up an ecstasy of his own, but he distances himself from it as though to say that such things do not dignify the status of one Christian over another (Harris 2005: 835; Matera 2003: 277; Furnish 1984: 544).

Some interpreters would go further, though, and argue that Paul may not have had any such experience at all. Instead, the heavenly journey of 2 Corinthians 12 is a fiction, possibly constructed from available literary resources, the goal of which is to parody the opponents' boasting about their own 'visions and revelations' (12.1; cf. Baird who is tempted by this reading, but, nevertheless, asserts that a 'fiction' would probably not silence Paul's opponents [1985: 659]). Jerry McCant, perhaps one of the most enthusiastic proponents of this approach, sees mocking parody everywhere he looks in this passage: '[T]he irony is that anyone who has returned from a heavenly experience without the evidence [after all, Paul can say nothing about it] should be so tempted to pride that God gives a "thorn in the flesh" to insure humility!' (1999: 144; drawing upon Betz 1972: 77-95). An interesting hybrid interpretation is that of Paula Gooder. Gooder agrees that Paul wants to validate Christian existence without recourse to special visions. And yet, Paul is also engaging in parody. She argues that Paul knows of traditions about mystical journeys, but that here he consciously critiques them by producing a flawed version, indeed, a 'subversion' of the traditional ascent genre (2006: 213); he does seem to have had the experience he describes, but it was a failure, as he was prevented from reaching higher than the third heaven by Satan (2006: 208). Gooder also notes, as do many, that the descent down the Damascus wall seems to have been intentionally paired by Paul with his heavenly ascent. In her view, though, this is a signal to the reader that we are dealing, in a doubly emphatic way, with the theme of weakness or failure rather than a more optimistic descent-ascent paradigm (2006: 167; for discussions of this paradigm see Thrall 2000: 764; Barrett 1997: 553).

However one chooses to understand Paul's account of this 'man's' ascent, it does seem eminently sensible to take the ironic tone of the larger context of 2 Corinthians 10–13 into account. This should be true not only of the heavenly journey, but of the 'thorn ... in the flesh, a messenger of Satan' (12.7). Gooder, as we just saw, considers the thorn to be a literary-metaphysical device to ensure the irony of Paul's boasting. The vast majority of interpretations, however, seek an actual, non-ironic, referent, not least because the thorn, while it formed part of Paul's visionary experience, apparently outlasts that experience in Paul's continuing 'weaknesses' (12.9-10), and weakness, rather than glory, is what makes his boasting so critically pointed. The explanations of just what condition Paul means are legion: anything from sexual temptation, to guilt or shame about aspects of his own work, to his opponents, to ailments physical—including epilepsy—and psychological (see the useful survey of scholarly conjecture in Thrall 2000: 809-818). Sandra Polaski's recent psychoanalytic reading, in something of a popular vein, is that Paul's thorn is so imprecisely defined because

Paul is referring to trauma, an experience that organizes the psyche around an inexplicable event, an event which language fails to capture (2008). This is a fascinating way of constructing religious experience, one that has as much in common with Dodd's 'second conversion', cited above, as with Slavoj Žižek's Lacanian theory. But, if the visionary ascent is parodic, as some maintain, then so is Paul's thorn, his Satanic messenger. McCant, who believes that thorn represents the minority of Corinthians with whom Paul has clashed, suggests that a healing story without a healing is necessarily parodic (1999: 151). The parody of the opponents, or of the minority faction's expectations of apostolic signs and wonders, becomes Christological irony as well as soon as we realize, McCant claims, that the three prayers and other details in the mini faux-healing narrative (12.7-10) are modeled on Jesus' passion (1999: 153; cf. Polaski 2008: 281-82). Although problematic, in that McCant turns Paul into a reader of the Gospels, consciously crafting his story in parallel with specific details from texts that post-date his ministry, his reading has two major advantages over others: first, it treats 2 Corinthians 12, very appropriately, as a sophisticated literary-rhetorical tour de force; and second, it eschews the elaborate archaeological labor required to get behind, or underneath, the text—when the text, of course, is all we have.

An interesting new area of research into Pauline personalia requires giving credence to material such as the heavenly journey in 2 Corinthians 12 in order to think about the embodied experience of faith. Colleen Shantz's work (2009), which reinvigorates an older history of religions approach to Paul, brings neuroscience into the conversation and examines Paul's language comparatively with studies of other recorded examples of altered states of consciousness.

Trash-Talkin' Fool

Much of the preceding discussion of the autobiographical material in 2 Corinthians has, by dint of the attention paid to Pauline parody, anticipated this section's focus on what is known as the Fool's Speech, the title Hans Windisch used for 2 Cor. 11.21–12.10 (1924: 349). Most scholars consider that the speech (or, less formally, discourse—Windisch's word is *Narrenrede*) begins at 11.1, with Paul's first use of 'foolishness', after which he paradoxically rejects and then accepts the title fool for himself (11.16-17), refers to the Corinthians' appreciation for fools (11.19), speaks as a fool (11.21) and a madman (11.23), once again sets aside the title of fool (12.6) before concluding, finally, that he has, indeed, been a fool after all (12.11). The general consensus is that the opponents' boasting (10.12-18; 11.12-13, 18, 21) and apparent lack of humility and/or scorn for Paul's apparent weaknesses and failures (10.1, 10; 11.7, 30; 12.7-10), having been well received in Corinth, elicit from Paul a bitterly defensive parody (11.16–12.13) designed to get the Corinthians to see him, to think of his apostolic role, with fresh eyes (10.7). As is evident from these citations, the start and finish of the Fool's Speech may be hard to pin down. If the escape from Damascus anecdote (11.30-33) is meant as an instance of foolish self-mockery, then Paul's strident military language in 10.3-6 might analogously be read as ludicrous, unreliable self-praise—Paul is paradoxically *both* the commander who storms citadels and the coward who flees under cover of night (Welborn 1999: 119; Furnish 1984: 542). We will return, below, to the martial rhetoric and its literary antecedents, but, for the moment, we should note that most readers tend to take Paul's imagery in 2 Corinthians 10 quite seriously, regardless of the 'meekness and gentleness of Christ' in Paul's appeal at 10.1. Frank Matera, for example, prefers to blame this tension between peace and violence in Paul's language on the Corinthians' own misunderstanding. They 'have not understood that in meekness and boldness, in clemency and battle, Paul is always the same' (2003: 223).

Whatever the textual boundaries of the Fool's Speech, it is obvious from Paul's language that something strange is afoot. Sharp irony and direct insult are common in Pauline polemic (e.g. Gal. 5.12; Phil. 3.2), so one is not surprised to find similar stuff here. Paul either believes that comparative boasting (2 Cor. 10.12) is foolish (and worse, 2 Cor. 10.18), or recognizes that the request (2 Cor. 13.3; cf. 12.12) that he likewise boast of his accomplishments would suggest his similarity to the very opponents he had been (foolishly?) criticizing. Possibly the opponents were labeling him a fool and he is responding in kind. Commentators usually adopt some combination of possible factors, with most also assuring us of Paul's noble purpose—he plays the fool only because it seems the surest way to rescue the Corinthians from the danger of losing faith. And this might be a fair description of Paul's own intentions.

But the various suggestions above still do not fully explain the extent of, the literary coherence of, this sustained, 'foolish' attack on the opposition. Paul could easily accuse the Corinthians or the opponents of folly without going to such great lengths to play the fool himself. An intriguing solution, proposed by Laurence Welborn, is that Paul, perhaps drawing upon personal experience as a set designer (a better translation, he contends, than 'tentmaker' in Acts 18.3 [2005: 11]), but, in any case, undoubtedly aware of the popularity of mimic fools, adapted characteristics of these stock types of the Greco-Roman mime tradition for his own ends. Mimes were performed as entertaining interludes between plays while sets were being changed in a traditional theater. One could see the mime nearly anywhere, though, as actors might appropriate a corner of the marketplace for a quick performance and a quick buck. Moreover, recognizable elements of the mime were also taken up in various literary texts. The mimic fool, then, was a widely available concept and would surely have been recognized by Paul's original readers (Welborn 1999: 127-31). Welborn argues that elements of the Fool's Speech, including especially the Damascus escape in 11.32-33, bear witness to this mime tradition. Like a jazz musician, as it were, Paul improvises a tune through mimic types—including the 'leading slave, [the] braggart warrior, [the] anxious old man', and 'the runaway fool' (1999: 131, 152). Each type involves characteristic behaviors and situations, and some-times the parallels cited by Welborn are quite similar indeed to what we find in Paul. The leading slave, for example, was known to boast of falsely glorious ancestries (see 2 Cor. 11.22; Welborn 1999: 139-40). The braggart soldier would boast of preposterous 'exploits and conquests' (see 11.24-27; Welborn 1999: 143). The anxious old man is a kind of Eeyore, complain-ing of, and suffering from, weaknesses and failures (see 11.28-29; Welborn 1999: 145-46). Even Paul's visionary ascent, Welborn argues, has its analog in mime and comedy, where 'the learned imposter' would boast of esoteric knowledge gained in heaven (1999: 148-49). The runaway fool is perhaps most intriguing since, as a literary category, it encompasses depictions of slaves, at one end of the social spectrum, and heroic figures like Odysseus, at the other. Odysseus's special-ops mission into Troy when he disguised himself as a beggar (*Odyssey* 4.240-64) is transformed in the mime's farci-cal mode into the story of a lying deserter who only wants to save his skin (Welborn 1999: 153). Paul, Welborn suggests, considered this caricature of his apostolic role in Corinth so significant that he intentionally placed it at the center of his Fool's Speech (1999: 157).

Developing catalogs of parallels is something of a pastime in the field and can lead to overdrawn conclusions, undoubtedly. But one extremely productive implication of a study of this kind is that Paul was in lively conversation with contemporary popular culture. He could rely upon his readers' familiarity with the fools of mime theater (much as a twenty-first century minister might call to mind characters in well-known films or from TV) as a way of commenting upon the performances of his opponents in Corinth. His suggestion would have been that his opponents compete for attention in the marketplace (see Georgi 1986 again) not only with other religious personalities, but also with mimic fools, and Paul leaves it to the Corinthians to draw their own conclusions about what such a shared com-petitive context might mean.

And yet Paul, also, is competing, fiercely so. For his part, he feels he is akin to God in his relationship with his children (12.14), who are like the first humans of Genesis 2–3 (11.2-3). We noted, in Chapter 3, that Paul damns his opponents as satanic ministers (11.14-15) and, in the Genesis parallel, these opponents become the cunning and deceptive serpent in the garden, which most take to be an additional suggestion of the devilishness of the opposition (e.g. Furnish 1984: 486). The choice, it seems, is obvious. It is also, and just as obviously, a polemically-charged choice, which the Corinthians may or may not have accepted. What is more, Paul's pretended folly, brilliant as it might be, incorporates a certain amount of violence. Welborn has shown that fools in the mime were often the victims of slapstick beatings, but their real-world counterparts—runaway slaves, for instance—courted severe physical assault. Something of the physical brutality associated with the mimic fool is directly hinted at by Paul who, in 11.19-20, accuses the Corinthians of 'gladly put[ting] up ... with it when someone makes slaves of you, or preys upon you, or takes advantage of you, or puts on airs, or gives you a slap in the face.' He is 'too weak for' doling out that sort of abuse, he says (11.21), but his opponents are not. Barrett, in a curious aside on these verses, notes that the opponents' intimidating tactics were in all likelihood 'gratifying ... [to] the Corinthians', 'so perverse is human nature' (1973: 292). It is a shame that Žižek's *The Puppet and The Dwarf: The Perverse Core of Christianity* (2003) doesn't mention Barrett's commentary (or this Pauline passage either), for they really are in intriguing conversation with one another with regard to the masochism to which they each allude. Be that as it may, Paul's accusation that the Corinthians gladly endure such abuse is most frequently taken metaphorically: no one is actually being slapped in the face. Welborn may consider the language figurative as well, but he links it to the mime, in which the fool really is publicly abused (1999: 151, quoting Chrysostom).

We have noted that violence is key to the Fool's Speech in other ways as well. Paul is a military commander laying siege to a city, destroying it and taking captives while also punishing those who fought against him (10.3-6; cf. Roetzel, where punishment becomes 'revenge' [2007: 98]). Even if Paul is simply appropriating tropes from Stoic and Cynic philosophical discourse (so Malherbe 1983), the fact remains that this entire section, 2 Corinthians 10–13, begins with siege imagery and concludes with the similarly martial threat of severe treatment, 'tearing down' (13.10). Given that we are dealing with the speech of a fool, Jeremy Punt, drawing upon postcolonial literary theory, argues that Paul's language of violence is catachrestic, that is, a 'subversive adaptation' of imperial or otherwise powerful and violent rhetorical strategies—perhaps even those of the Cynics and Stoics—a 'strategic misrepresentation' that upends power through parody (2008: 277). On the other hand, Paul may be using such imagery in all seriousness, thereby suggesting that his response to the Corinthian situation will be a violent one. In fact, Graham Shaw takes an approach quite opposite to that of Punt, with reference to this context, for he sees an incipient imperialism in

10.16—Paul's bid for universal, unchallenged authority 'in lands beyond ...
someone else's sphere of action' (1983: 120). Paul brooks 'no independent
source of power in the communities which he has founded' (1983: 121).
Shaw's unflinching critique of authority in the New Testament is really quite
scathing towards Paul, '[F]or all his talk of weakness and identification with
the cross, it is by no means clear that he stands with the crucified. There is a
horrid suspicion that he ultimately stands with those who were prepared to
crucify in order to defend and preserve their position. In this the Christian
Paul is not perhaps so different from the persecuting Saul' (1983: 125).
Shaw's critics accuse him of partial readings or anachronistic analysis, but
their responses frequently sound less like discussions of methodology than
apologies for Paul. Margaret Thrall, for example, who does make an effort
to take Shaw's criticism seriously, ultimately defends what seems to be violence and exclusivity in Paul by arguing that these are merely 'the negative
converse of positive qualities vitally necessary' for his 'calling as apostle'
(2000: 959; cf. Polaski 1999: 17-18). But Shaw is certainly not alone in taking issue with the violence of Paul's images in 2 Corinthians. Calvin Roetzel
characterizes 10.1-6 as 'a savage and ugly brew of war metaphors', the aim
of which is 'to coerce, to silence dissent, to control speech and thought,
to subdue, to humiliate and to dominate' (2010: 79, 91). More positively,
Roetzel believes that, immediately upon expressing himself in these terms,
Paul 'squirms' in discomfort at his own bellicose rhetoric (Roetzel 2007:
99). It is even possible that the Fool's Speech is a direct result of this discomfort, that Paul was so surprised by his own brutality that he begins, at
least, to 'reframe the whole nature of power' and is, himself, 'transformed'
by his portrayal of the weaknesses of the fool (Roetzel 2010: 95).

The transformation is not entirely successful, as Paul begins to bluster
again in 2 Corinthians 13. Even before that, Paul remains vitriolic in reject-
ing his opponents, as we have seen. Moreover, many would point to the
reference to Eve in 11.2-3 as deeply problematic, not only for contemporary
readers, but for Paul's original audience as well. Shelly Matthews contrasts
the significance of women's vitality in the religious life of 1 Corinthians with
their reduction to a metaphor of licentiousness in this passage—the entire
community is, like Eve, vulnerable to the seductions of the intruders (1993:
212). As commentators note, the metaphor develops very traditional concepts pertaining to Israel's relationship with God, a relationship understood
in marital terms (e.g. Isa. 54.5-6 [Furnish 1984: 499]). And Paul's Eve can
be read in different ways, even among feminists. David Scholer claims that
Paul includes the whole church in Eve, extending her guilt to men and
women equally, rather than limiting culpability to women alone, as in the
Pastorals (1 Tim. 2.14 [Scholer 2003: 114]). The distinction between 2
Corinthians and Pseudo-Pauline misogyny may be a useful one, but it is still

troubling to many readers that Paul genders the whole community this way and takes for himself the role of the *paterfamilias*, who is responsible for his daughter's sexuality, and thus can dispose of it as he wishes (e.g. Schüssler Fiorenza 2007: 85; cf. Thrall 2000: 661 on Paul's role as father). Unlike Scholer, Elizabeth Schüssler Fiorenza actually sees continuity between Paul and 1 Timothy. She argues that 2 Corinthians is partially responsible for a later tradition demanding women's subordination and blaming women for their own victimization (2011: 112).

The need to recognize and deal forthrightly with Pauline politics—of gender, of apostolic authority—does not prevent us from identifying and, even celebrating, the intimate, unguarded expressions of affection in 2 Corinthians. We have alluded several times already to the change in tone between 1 Corinthians and 2 Corinthians. In 1 Corinthians, Paul refers to his audience as brothers ('brothers and sisters' NRSV) no less than twenty times and in 2 Corinthians only thrice (1.8; 8.1; 13.11). But they are still beloved (1 Cor. 4.14; 10.14; 15.58; 2 Cor. 7.1; 12.19; cf. 2.4; 11.11; 12.15), they are still his boast (1 Cor. 15.31; 2 Cor. 1.14; 7.4, 14; 8.24; 9.2-4), and he still wants to be joined to them in sincere communion (1 Cor. 12–13; 2 Cor. 4.14; 6.11-12; 7.2-3; 10.15-16). Although, as readers, we may dislike the paternalism implied in some of these passages, we should give Paul credit, as Murray Harris does, when he seems genuinely to desire participation with the Corinthians in mutual love, the intensity of which would be shared equally and joyfully by all (2005: 887-88).

5

THEOLOGICAL INSIGHTS

Paul never got to travel the dusty roads of Spain, to notice its curvaceous slopes and the busyness of its coastal life, because he died a martyr's death in Rome. The story of Paul's life is the story, the tragic story, of unfulfilled hopes and shattered dreams.

—Martin Luther King, Jr. 'Unfulfilled Hopes'

No Pain, No Gain

Even while acknowledging the polemical foundations of Paul's rhetoric and, hence, the self-serving nature of many of his assertions, we cannot fail to notice, and be moved by, the significance of suffering in 2 Corinthians. The letter begins with the need for consolation in the face of affliction and suffering, and it ends with a reminder of Paul's own Christ-like weakness (13.9). Other concepts no less important get cameos in discussions of the letter's theology, but suffering (weakness, despair) takes center stage.

As is the case with the epistolary openings in Paul's other letters, with the exception of Galatians, the initial verses after the salutation in 2 Corinthians function like a thanksgiving, even though the typical language of thanks (e.g. 1 Thess. 2.10) is absent. Several factors probably contribute to the fact that Paul speaks of blessings rather than thankfulness—his own rescue from death (1.8-11); his relief that the tensions between himself and the community have abated (7.5-7); and his conflict with rival missionaries who bring a message of glory and strength (10.10; 12.11-12). As a result, some choose to name 1.3-11 a blessing section (e.g. Furnish 1984: 116), while others refer to it as a thanksgiving (e.g. Barrett 1973: 57) or use both terms without taking a position on the matter (e.g. Roetzel 2007: 127). However one designates the literary genre of these verses, they are critical to Paul's message. Paul blesses God, 'the father of our Lord Jesus Christ, the father of mercies and the God of all consolation' (1.3). That Paul is here adapting the language of contemporary Jewish worship is remarked upon by all commentators. Not explicitly noted, however, is the importance of 1.5 for understanding 1.3 (but see Kruse 2008: 62). The chiasmus in 1.3,

'God, Father' and then 'Father, God', has an echo in the near-chiasmus (Furnish 1984: 118; cf. Lim 2009: 42) of 1.5—'Christ's suffering, us' and then 'our consolation, Christ'—so that Christ needs to be understood in the earlier verse not only in association with God's mercies and consolation, but also with affliction (1.4). Indeed, somehow, as the *source* of affliction as in 'the sufferings of Christ are abundant for us' (1.5; 'overflowing to us' in Furnish 1984: 108). Readers have puzzled over how Paul may experience 'the sufferings of Christ'. Common solutions are: that Paul, in experiencing physical traumas, essentially imitates Jesus' earthly sufferings (e.g. Moss 2010: 27; Murphy-O'Connor 1991: 143; Hooker 1981: 78); that Paul sees suffering as part of the tribulations attendant upon the last times (Barrett 1973: 61-2); and, that Paul believes in something of an actual or 'realistic' participation in Christ's *own* suffering (Proudfoot 1963). The third of these options, sometimes in combination with the second (despite the uncertain applicability of 'messianic woes' to Pauline thought, see Lim 2009: 45-48; Thrall 2000; 107-108), represents the current consensus. The sufferings of Christ are mystically extended to later Christians who participate in Christ by experiencing them (e.g. Campbell 2009: 354; Wan 2000: 36-37; Thrall 1994: 108-109; Segal 1990: 68). The nature of this participation is necessarily difficult to describe, but some, like Furnish, consider it to be grounded in the idea that the Christian community is Christ's mystical body (1984: 120). Other Pauline passages, particularly Phil. 3.10 and Rom. 6.3-6, are cited in corroboration of the general notion, and Col. 1.24 is said to provide some further specific indication that Christians, continuing Christ's bodily existence, must complete his sufferings (Dunn 2006: 486; Harris 2005: 146). An important alternative possibility is that by 'the sufferings of Christ' Paul has in mind not simply Jesus' passion, but his entire ministry, since Jesus also 'had to suffer persecution and rejection in his mission' (Lim 2009: 52). Although it is hardly satisfying to read Paul's specific references to Jesus' death as merely metonymic (2009: 110; cf. Hafemann 2000: 109), taking a broader view of missiological trials would help link such lesser Pauline difficulties as 'perplexity' (4.8) and 'anxiety' (11.28) to the overall theme of Christ-like affliction.

We have seen how Paul, in 2 Corinthians 10–13, harps upon his sufferings and weakness in order to contrast his apostolate from that of the rival missionaries. He clearly also strikes the same chord in 2 Corinthians 1–7. The sufferings of Christ (1.5) are experienced in the human bodies of believers, 'clay jars' (4.7) which bear the treasure of the gospel message, but which also make manifest in their frailty 'the death of Jesus' (4.10). And the Christian, in this case, specifically, Paul, is also 'always le[d] ... in triumphal procession' (2.14). The imagery of the triumph recalls the processions associated with the homecoming of victorious Roman military leaders. Triumphal processions typically included a host of captured soldiers destined for execution (see the vivid summary of literary accounts of triumphs in Roetzel 2007: 55-59). Paul seems to imply that he is just such a captive, an image disturbing to many in its implications. Various alternative readings have, therefore, been proposed. Most famously, in English, the King James Bible reads the verb *thriambeuō* in a causative sense: 'causeth us to triumph'. Contemporary scholars find this reading, which goes back at least to Calvin (Hafemann 2000: 107-108), improbable. Perhaps it is possible, as Calvin proposed, that Paul imagines himself as one of God's subordinate commanders after a successful battle (so Barrett 1973: 98; Aus 2005: 17-20). Most scholars, however, try to take the image in its most common sense. If the triumph, a word used only here and at Col. 2.15 in the New Testament, is an indication of God's victorious power over his defeated foes, then quite possibly Paul has in mind his conversion, when God took captive the persecutor of the church and now displays him, a prisoner or slave of Christ (so Stegman 2009: 72; Matera 2003: 72; Hafemann 2000: 109). Perhaps, having been spared death, Paul the captive former foe was placed under an obligation to serve as Christ's ambassador (5.20; Matera 2003: 72-3). Readings such as these tend to reference Paul's many allusions to suffering and service elsewhere in the Corinthian correspondence in order to contextualize the image of the triumph. But the image itself remains a problem for some, who, as a result, will occasionally opt for a minimalist interpretation—Paul is merely indicating God's glory (Thrall 1994: 195); Paul is simply drawing attention to his weaknesses (Furnish 1984: 187). Some note that, among Hellenistic writers, the triumph could be adapted metaphorically and suggest that this is what Paul is doing (so McCant, for whom Paul may be thinking polemically and in Senecan terms about patronage [1999: 34]). A brilliant metaphorical reading, mentioned already in Chapter 2, has been elaborated by Paul Duff, who surveys literary uses of the triumph image before settling on one that makes the most sense of Paul: '[A]lthough Paul might look like he is being "led in triumph", a victim of defeat, the object of the vengeance of God, he is in fact a captive of the "love of Christ"' (1991: 87) in an epiphany procession, which could closely resemble a triumph. This is a 'parody' of the criticism that Paul's weaknesses and failures mark him as a victim of God's wrath (Duff 1991: 87). Duff sees the metaphor extending throughout this section of the letter. Accordingly, he reinterprets the clay jars in 4.7 as the vessels in an epiphany procession that carried the deity's sacred objects or images. That Paul's body is the clay jar helps make additional sense of 4.10, where 'carrying in the body the death of Jesus' becomes a sign of God's saving activity (Duff 1991: 88). Indeed, 4.10, structurally similar to 2.14, is what redefines the earlier verse and so re-characterizes the nature of the triumph—as not a military procession, but a public festival celebrating the return of the deity to the deity's temple. When later, in 6.11 and 7.2, Paul requests that the Corinthians 'open [their] hearts', he does so as a herald of the procession (Duff 1991: 88-90; cf. Duff 1993, which makes 6.14–7.1 essential to this reading).

Duff, like some scholars discussed in Chapter 2, believes that 2 Cor. 2.14–7.4 (perhaps excluding 6.14–7.1) is an independent letter fragment. It is unclear whether his corroborating sources (which take this fragment as an initial and milder appeal than the later vitriolic letter of tears) indicate anything about how he himself would reconstruct the epistolary sequence. But his reading leaves one wondering how the martial imagery of 10.3-6 is to be understood. Whether or not Paul's transformation into a military commander in 2 Corinthians 10 is ironic parody, it might logically be a retort to critical commentary on his earlier self-depiction as herald in an epiphany procession; that is, perhaps after receiving the letter now contained in the fragment under discussion, Paul's Corinthian critics opted to *misread* that image, casting Paul not as a herald, but as vanquished captive. Margaret Mitchell rightly praises Duff as the scholar who has 'best understood and explicated' the hermeneutic workings of 2 Cor. 2.14–7.4, but neither she nor Duff takes up the possibility of a connection between 2.14 and 10.3-6. Similarly, the broader cultural hermeneutics need some explication as well. How can Paul re-imagine his apostleship in terms of a pagan religious procession without risking the difficult resolution of the problem concerning food sacrificed to idols from 1 Corinthians 8–10? Still, even in raising these additional questions, Duff's work extends our appreciation for Paul's grasp of the cultural resources available to him. And it forces us to rethink some basic assumptions about the significance of suffering in Pauline theology.

This Mortal Coil

Suffering, however, is but one side of the equation, and arguably the less important side at that, for it is always overcome by consolation (e.g. 1.3-7). Grief gives way to salvation (7.10), pain to perfection (12.7-9), death to life (1.9-10; 4.10; 5.14-15; cf. 2.15-16; 3.6). And some of the most theologically fertile material in 2 Corinthians can be read as Paul's concluding reflections, in this portion of the epistle at least, upon the productive use and ultimate overcoming of suffering. 2 Corinthians 5.1–6.2 includes what appears to be enigmatic reflection upon the body's spiritual transformation upon death or at the *eschaton*, the meaning of Christ's sacrifice, and the participation in Christ as a new creation. All of this follows close upon the heels of 4.7-18, which suggests that 2 Corinthians 5 explores the same renewal and glory presumed in the necessary suffering of Christians like Paul. Indeed, commentaries will sometimes treat 4.7–5.10 as a unit in its own right, with 4.16-18 being especially significant for the complicated theological expressions of 2 Corinthians 5. From one perspective, these verses at the end of 2 Corinthians 4 merely further the suffering-consolation dynamic with which the letter begins, and they seem to do so with a hint of polemic (e.g. 4.18 may try to characterize complaints about Paul's hardships and weaknesses as superficial thinking). But the contrast between the inner and outer person ('nature' NRSV) in 4.16 intrigues many readers, to a large extent because Paul's anthropology is usually not considered dualistic, and yet, here, we seem to have a dualism with Platonic roots (see the excellent discussion of Paul's 'inner man' idea in Betz 2000). Typically in Paul, the human being consists of 'spirit and soul and body' (1 Thess. 5.23). The latter concept, the body, can seem dualistic—it is either *sarx* or *soma*—but both are essentially human. The church, as the *body* of Christ, is *soma* (1 Cor. 12.27) not *sarx*. In fact, *sarx* is opposed to God's law (Rom. 7.5). Nevertheless, in a passage from Philippians that resembles the material under consideration here, Paul uses both terms to describe an embodied, earthly life in service to Christ and to the church (1.20-24), so even this dualism, if that is the best way to describe it (Thrall is likewise ambivalent [1994: 351]), is imperfect. The same can be said of the inner and outer person. Clearly, there is a tension between the two, for the former is 'wasting away', while the latter 'is being renewed day by day', but the outer person is not thereby denigrated or even completely subordinated to the inner. Even if the outer person is the frail clay jar of 2 Cor. 4.7, it (he/she?) is still the vehicle for making 'the life of Jesus ... visible' (4.10; cf. 12.9). It is precisely by experiencing affliction in the body that the Christian is prepared for eternal glory (4.17). At the same time, the inner person is also not yet fully developed, for only slowly, day by day, does it experience renewal (cf. 5.5; 3.18).

Paul goes on to express his confident knowledge that 'if the earthly tent we live in is destroyed, we have a building from God, a house not made with hands, eternal in the heavens' (5.1). Mixing metaphors, he then re-characterizes these dwellings as clothing to be put on or removed (5.2-4). The most straightforward explanation, and the one adopted by most commentators, is that the body is the earthly tent (cf. Wis. 9.19; 2 Pet. 1.13-14) and the heavenly house is the spirit-embodiment of the believer at the resurrection. Verse 1 is not ideally straightforward, however, because the scenario is described in a conditional sense, '*if* the earthly tent ... is destroyed'. Some scholars choose a psychologically focused exegesis at this point, reasoning that, especially after the crisis in Asia (1.8), Paul now must come to terms with the possibility that he will die before the *parousia* (so Harris 2005: 380; Thrall 1994: 563; Barrett 1973: 156). Earlier,

Paul had felt that he would certainly see the coming of the Lord (1 Thess. 4.15; 1 Cor. 15). Now circumstances require him to determine more precisely what happens to those who die before the *eschaton*. Accordingly, the language of nakedness (5.3-4) is read as an expression of Paul's anxiety (almost a horror, in Barrett 1973: 154-56) at the possibility that he might lose his earthly body to the grave for a period before finally receiving his resurrection body at Christ's return. Nakedness, in this sense, is disembodiment, which had encouraged earlier readers to imagine that Paul is denying here a gnostic hope for a spiritual future free from material encumbrance (e.g. Bultmann 2007: 169). Most contemporary scholars reject this view (but see Harris 2005: 389), although some accept that Paul might be countering more general Hellenistic dualism of the spirit/body type (Furnish 1984: 300-301). Most also believe that the nudity of 5.3 is not a reference to the moral status of the opponents, or unbelievers, even though this interpretation is possible (see the discussion in Thrall 1994: 375-76, 378-79). The consensus is that Paul is speculating on what happens to Christians post-mortem, but pre-resurrection. The most hopeful supposition is that Paul believes in 'the ideal possession of the spiritual body at death with real possession at the parousia' (Harris 2005: 380). Despite the reassurance such a notion might provide, Paul, like the world itself in Rom. 8.22, groans with longing to be present at the end of creation, to have his mortality suddenly 'swallowed up by life' (5.4).

Not all readers are convinced by this. Victor Furnish, for instance, is hard-pressed to find any reason to think that Paul is here discussing only obliquely what he speaks of so directly in 1 Thessalonians 4 and 1 Corinthians 15. What is more, the crisis in Asia, Furnish thinks, far from leading Paul into morbid depression, is a major source of his optimism and confidence (1.10-11; 1984: 293). This text is not a 'thanatology', then, but part of Paul's ongoing discussion of suffering and consolation. And, throughout it, we find exactly the same dual vision, in which the afflictions of the present are contrasted with the hope of the future (e.g. 4.10-14, 17-18; 5.5-9). The eternal, heavenly home is not the spiritual body, but rather the apocalyptic New Jerusalem, reminiscent of 2 Esd. 10.40-57; Paul, here, and in Phil. 3.12-21 (cf. Phil. 1.29–2.1), reminds his readers that, though they dwell on earth in suffering, they really, 'and thus in a decisive sense already, belong to another age' (1984: 295; cf. Roetzel 2007: 75-77). After all, as Paul will put it in a moment, 'now is the day of salvation' (6.2). Although the consensus reading may be perfectly valid, and although critics of a similar stripe seem reasonable to understand the heavenly dwelling as the resurrection body and not the new Jerusalem (e.g. Woodbridge 2003: 257-58), Furnish's interpretation makes perfect sense of the passage in view of Paul's rhetorical need to show that his suffering is in itself evidence of his apostolic authenticity.

All commentators agree that such is Paul's message. But many seem temporarily to forget the importance of this theme when it comes to the next major image related, however loosely, to the inner/outer person of 4.16. Paul makes another (semi-dualistic) distinction, 'while we are at home in the body we are away from the Lord' (5.6). Being with the Lord would then mean being away from the body, presumably the wasting, earthly tent, rather than the resurrection body. Barrett, throughout this section of his commentary, agrees with Paul as only an ardent ascetic might, for he feels that 'it is well to be rid of' the body; 'the only possible reaction of the Christian to the present age is that he should die to it' by means of 'union with Christ' (1973: 151-52). Paul, too, acknowledges his readiness to leave the body behind (5.8). But there is something hasty about his language here. In Barrett's view, Paul's anacolouthic stumble (represented in the NRSV by a dash, as though Paul were pausing mid-thought) is evidence of a sudden awareness that he has just said something incorrect, that Christians are absent from Christ while alive (1973: 158). In Furnish's view, 'Paul is not entirely pleased with the ... antithesis' (1984: 302). Thrall senses that 'Paul's mood changes', improves really, since he has left behind the morose thought of a disembodied (or, more properly, a physically corrupting) hiatus in his faithful existence. But the confidence of 5.6 leads, in her reading as well, to language that is not as theologically sound as it should be (1994: 385-86). Perhaps the reason for the awkward break between 5.6 and 5.7 is that Paul is citing a slogan from some faction of the opposition in Corinth which he could use to forestall any misunderstanding of his tent imagery (Murphy-O'Connor 2010: 106), or which he wants to correct by 'radically altering' it (Furnish 1984: 303). The alteration involves a change in prepositions. 'In the body' and 'with the Lord' of 5.6 now become, albeit in inverted form, 'away from the body' and 'toward the Lord' (1984: 274), an adjustment signaling orientation rather than location (Furnish 1984: 302). Of course, the absence of the markers he uses elsewhere to signal a citation of this kind (e.g. 'now concerning' in 1 Cor. 8.1) is one reason for caution in accepting this interpretation (Harris 2005: 395). Most commentators agree that he is not now speaking in favor of disembodiment but rather is focusing on faithful Christian existence (5.7, 9) with an eye toward the coming judgment (5.10) and union with the Lord. Ultimately, whether or not Paul is citing anyone at this point, he may still be goading his readers with polemic, contrasting his faithful ministry to one committed to showy manifestations of authenticity (4.18; 5.7, 12).

The verbs Paul uses for being 'at home' and 'away', which appear only here in the Greek scriptures, can mean 'being with one's people' or 'a native', and 'being abroad' or 'in exile', respectively. Given the increasing prominence of postcolonial approaches to the New Testament, it surely will not be long before there is a thorough study of the conceptual function of exile in these verses.

New and Improved!

There is already significant alternative interest in one of Paul's most fascinating theological ideas, the 'new creation' of 2 Cor. 5.17 (cf. Gal. 6.15). Holly Hearon, in *The Queer Bible Commentary*, writes that the new creation is the hope for a future in which 'racism, gender-privilege, internalized homophobia, economic disparity and deprivation' have been 'shattered, just like clay jars' (2006: 260-61). For Theodore Jennings, the new creation is linked to Christ's identification with the oppressed—he reads 'sin' in 5.21 as exclusion or marginalization (2009: 99)—and so as social rather than individual: 'it is something that takes place in and through history, a history that is public and, indeed, political ... the messianic life [of the new creation] is a life that renounces self-preoccupation in order to live in openness and vulnerability with others, and so enables the appearance of a new form of messianic sociality in which justice, peace, and joy may be actualized' (2009: 196-97). Matthew Lowe, in an unpublished paper, imagines Paul's ambassadorial role in contemporary geopolitical terms. Paul and his 'ambassadors for Christ' (5.20), Lowe writes, 'are called to be transnational delegates of a transnational God, the giver of grace and a reconciling ministry that heralds God's new creation and extends a welcome to the exiled and the stateless' (2011: 11). The intention here is evidently to empower the marginalized, even if the imagery involved suggests a kind of divine global governance. Aliou Cissé Niang takes a similar approach, but with a critical difference, reading Paul as 'a sociopostcolonial hermeneut and countercolonist sent by Jesus Christ/God to create a new and inclusive community whose members are conscious of their new status and prerogatives as socioreligious beings' (2007: 138; Niang focuses more specifically on Gal. 6.15). Elizabeth Schüssler Fiorenza reads this verse as a sort of political marker both in the contemporary academic study of Paul and in the world of Paul's Corinth, distinguishing two very clear paths: on the one side, the new creation, an 'alternative society', and on the other, 'those who legitimate the patriarchal structures and imperialist values of Greco-Roman society in ideological terms' (2000: 51).

The political valence of this verse, its importance for readings of a hopeful theological stripe, is tremendous, and I could go on citing texts like those above. Even in less politically engaged readings, the hopeful possibilities of the verse can abound as well. A recent study by T. Ryan Jackson resorts, at times, to fairly exuberant language—Christ's cross is 'the epicentre of God's cosmic earthquake' (2010: 129)—in the process of emphasizing the range of possible meanings for Paul's new creation. Jackson argues that Paul has recourse both to Jewish texts (Isaianic and later apocalyptic sources) and to the idea of new creation in Roman imperial ideology in his totalizing view of the change wrought by Christ's death and resurrection. Paul's soteriology, as articulated here, includes the renovation of all being: '[T]he individual convert ... is a microcosm of the ultimate act of redemption which God plans for the entire cosmos' (Jackson 2010: 148). The social order is necessarily included in so all-encompassing an idea of reconciliation, especially in Roman Corinth, where 'new creation' would have been heard in the context of an imperial ideology, the political 'soteriology [of which] was cosmological in nature' (Jackson 2010: 66). Jackson further notes that creation [*ktisis*] could refer to the founding of cities (2010: 65). In a very real and multivocal sense, Corinth itself, as a social entity, would thus be a new creation. If its public monuments and architecture reflected the new world order of Rome, and if Paul's community in Corinth were as well-versed in imperial ideology as one might expect, then his theme in this passage would reverberate for them in a variety of intriguing ways (Jackson 2010: 148-49). Jackson, unfortunately, does not spend a great deal of time thinking through the specific politics of new creation in Corinth. Wary of imposing a subversive, anti-imperial reading upon Paul, the most he will say is that Paul's audiences would probably have been aware that Paul's new creation implied 'a radically different understanding of world transformation' than that of Rome (2010: 63).

His broad focus, however, is of a piece with other readings that take Paul's commitment to social (as above) and cosmic transformation seriously (e.g. see Sigfred Pedersen who takes 5.17 as evidence that the law, for Paul, is never the Mosaic covenant, but always the 'creation commandment' of Gen. 2.15-17 and related texts [2002: 29]). This marks a significant contrast with more standard readings, which tend to take new creation to signify a relatively bland and politically neutral ethical adjustment. Building upon his comment in 5.16, that Christians need to understand others in a new, spiritual light, many commentators assume that Paul is speaking, in 5.17, about a kind of present inner renewal which will only have its outer reality in the eschatological future (Roetzel 2007: 81; Harris 2005: 432; Matera 2003: 135-56; Thrall 1994: 427-28; Furnish 1984: 332-33; Barrett 1973: 173-74). These commentators note, and variously accept the relevance of, sources Paul might have in mind, such as Isaiah 49 (cited by Paul in 6.2) and Isa. 65.17-19. But the apocalyptic dimension is usually cast in the idiom of personal transformation. The new creation is a way of understanding God's reconciliation with 'us' (5.19), and the anthropological reading is, admittedly, faithful to the whole of 5.17a: 'if *anyone* is in Christ, there is a new creation'. But an exclusive focus on the individual believer, even if in the context of other Christians, can have the unfortunate effect of pacifying the desire for actual change to which the citations in the previous paragraph attest. Indeed, as Ralph Martin puts it, this reconciliation is completely *passive* from the human (and grammatical) perspective; Christians are 'acted upon' by being 'reconciled' and then 'appealed to' (1987: 108). Paul's language surely supports this view, since it is God 'who reconciled us to himself' (5.18). Scriptural parallels in 2 Maccabees (e.g. 8.29) are, in fact, rather different, as they envision reconciliation with God that is initiated by believers. In Paul, however, even the appeal to believers that they 'be reconciled to God', is likewise a denial of substantial agency; Paul is merely asking the Corinthians to respond to God's initiative positively (Thrall 1994: 438), or 'to acknowledge the presence of a "new creation"' (Furnish 1984: 350). Theologically, it can be said that Christ's own function was precisely passivity, passive obedience, either in undergoing God's wrath in place of guilty humanity (as in Anselm's theory of atonement; cf. Rom. 6.23), or in being made a cultic sin-offering (as in 1 Cor. 5.7; cf. Lev 4–5.13; Isa. 53; Heb. 4.14–10.31). A good many interpreters believe that the former, satisfaction model of atonement is most pertinent to these verses; consequently, 'becom[ing] the righteousness of God' in 5.21 has a juridical sense, and means being declared just, being cleared of guilt, in God's eyes.

The passivity of the sacrificial Christ has long been a problem for feminists and other readers attentive to the dangers—for women, but also for all who are marginal to power, 'the crucified peoples' (Reid 2007: 4)—of valorizing obedience in suffering. Catholic readings of this righteousness can involve a more active participation, an empowerment, among believers (see Stegman 2009: 145), even if Christ's experience is still that of the passive sufferer. Sometimes a certain passivity can be part of the solution. God's gift in Christ, argues Barbara Reid in *Taking up the Cross: New Testament Interpretation through Latina and Feminist Eyes*, is love, and love ought to take precedence over sin and punishment in discussions of atonement. Perhaps more significantly, one can read agency back into ambiguous Pauline verses, like 2 Cor. 5.20. Most contemporary commentaries assume that Paul's first person plural here, 'we are ambassadors of Christ', signifies, at most, the apostles, or Paul himself along with his co-workers; some commentators are uncomfortable with the way the Pauline embassy would have constituted a power play, 'pure and simple', for anyone mistreating an ambassador courted 'extreme peril' (Roetzel 2007: 82). Still, for Reid, all believers are ambassadors of Christ, reciprocating God's generosity while simultaneously evading the sheer passivity of divine grace (2007: 132; cf. Stegman 2009: 146; Harris also thinks it probable that 'through us' in this verse includes 'all proclaimers of reconciliation' [2005: 447]).

Theodore Jennings, by translating righteousness as justice, similarly creates the opportunity for a more direct participation in the new creation and
the righteousness it entails. Jennings has consistently linked Paul's Jesus
with criminality, or, more precisely, with the status of an outlaw, someone
whose exclusion from legal privileges—understood very broadly to include
all legal codes and the violence inherent in them (2006: 56)—is fully evident in his execution. He is an outsider to the law, in the way that an
undocumented worker or a political activist can be. But, as such, Paul's
Jesus is also 'the bearer of justice' and this on the basis of 2 Cor. 5.21: 'so
that we might become the justice of God' (2006: 66). Jennings conceives
of the Pauline community as those 'who are in solidarity with [the] mes-
siah; that is ... [those] for whom [the Christ] event is exemplary or who are
exemplified by that event' (2006: 67). It is worth noting in this regard that
Martin Luther King, Jr. when he was called an extremist in Birmingham,
Alabama, retorted that he was in good company, for so was Paul, specifically
the Paul of Gal. 6.17, who said 'I bear in my body the marks of the Lord
Jesus' (King 1992: 94).

N.T. Wright's intriguing (and controversial; cf. Piper 2007) interpretation of 'righteousness of God' in 2 Cor. 5.21 doesn't necessarily address the
problem of passivity, but it circumvents the judicial sense discussed above,
and, therefore, may avoid readings which model, as Reid puts it, 'manipu-
lative cycles of guilt and gratitude' (2007: 30). In Romans, righteousness
always refers to God's fidelity to the covenant, according to Wright. In fact,
righteousness means God's covenant faithfulness. Wright does not treat 2
Cor. 5.21 as an exception to this rule, as though Paul were referring here
and only here to a quality imputed to believers by God. The verses following 5.14-15, Wright argues, are essentially recapitulations of that important
creedal statement: Christ died for all and we live (read: engage in ministry)
for him. The summation of this logic is 5.21, which is the logic of much of
2.14–6.13, namely that Christ died (as sin), so that 'we might *embody God's
faithfulness, God's covenant faithfulness, God's action in reconciling the world
to himself*' (2009: 163; italics original). The focus here is on the nature of
apostleship—'the deeply subversive theology of Christian ministry' (Wright
2009: 164)—and not the salvation status of believers.

Money in the Bank

Finally, we turn to 2 Corinthians 8 and 9. Whatever their order and literary
relationship to one another, these texts open an interesting window into
Paul's ministry. The collection for the Jerusalem church is ostensibly just a
pragmatic matter. The Corinthians have not completed their fundraising
activities yet, and Paul clearly wants to ensure that they will do so, in short

order, thus enabling him to combine their gift with the donated funds from the Macedonian churches and to deliver the whole amount to Jerusalem. According to Rom. 15.25-28, both Achaia and Macedonia were 'pleased to share their resources with the poor among the saints' of the mother church. The Gentiles 'owe it to' the original Jewish community of Jesus' followers, he adds, because it is only through the latter that the former have experienced 'spiritual blessings' (Rom. 15.27). It is uncertain whether or not Paul was ever able to deliver his collection to Jerusalem or, if he did, whether or not it was accepted. That Paul was in doubt about the success or otherwise of the whole enterprise is evident from his prayer, a few verses on in Romans, that he 'may be rescued from the unbelievers in Judea, and that [his] ministry to Jerusalem may be acceptable to the saints' (Rom. 15.31).

This would be a strange anxiety if Paul's collection were undertaken at the behest of the Jerusalem church itself, which is not impossible. In Gal. 2.10, Paul reports that he had been asked by 'the acknowledged pillars'—James, Peter, and John—to 'remember the poor' and that he 'was eager to do' so. The rest of Galatians is unconcerned with the collection, but, in 1 Cor. 16.1, Paul advises the Corinthians to follow the procedure for gathering gifts of money that he established in the Galatian churches. 2 Corinthians 8–9 deals extensively with the recent history of the Corinthian effort (8.6, 10; 9.2), the participation of the Macedonian churches (8.1-5; 9.1, 4), the delegates overseeing the collection (8.6, 16-23; 9.3-5), and, most importantly for us here, the way this gift will shape their relationship with Jerusalem (8.13-15; 9.12-14). Obviously, then, Paul both acknowledges his commitment to, and actually carries out, a fund-raising ministry for the poor in Jerusalem (but Georgi argues that 'poor' here designates a special religious status rather than a state of financial need [1991: 37-38]). The Jerusalem conference narrated in Acts 15 does not make mention of an agreement concerning the collection. But Acts 11.27-30 has Barnabas and Paul delivering funds from Antioch to aid 'the believers in Judea' during, or in advance of, a predicted famine. Although it is narrated earlier, is this Paul's collection?

Many interpreters see a direct connection between the Jerusalem conference and Paul's collection (e.g. Roetzel 2007: 39; Matera 2003: 182; Joubert 2000: 6; Furnish 1984: 410). Some, however, argue that the collection Paul refers to in Galatians pertained specifically to Antioch's relationship with Jerusalem and that after Paul and Cephas clashed, and after he and Barnabas had their falling out and Paul departed on a ministry of his own (Gal. 2.13; Acts 15.36-41), he was no longer obligated to participate (e.g. Downs 2008: 35; Thrall 2000: 506). Readings such as these must necessarily explain why Paul undertakes a collection anyway, and they usually do so by alluding to goals Paul crafts on the model, but independently, of the collection agreement between Jerusalem and Antioch. We will discuss some of these aims below as they tend to be theologically significant—at least most of these reconstructions do. Jerome Murphy-O'Connor, without excluding basic humanitarian and generally religious goals, also suggests that Paul might have undertaken his own version of the collection in order 'to pour burning coals on the head of his enemies' (à la Rom. 12.20; 1996: 145). The pillars in Jerusalem would certainly be put in an uncomfortable position by a strong show of (much-needed) material support from the Gentile Christians they had repudiated. A variation on this reading, one requiring less justification, holds that Paul was *already* engaged in a ministry of assistance to the poor—taking Gal. 2.10 to indicate that Paul was just reaffirming a prior commitment of his own—and, thus, that he was already acting independently of any request from the pillars (Harris 2005: 89). Luke's only other mention of a fund-raising function in Paul's ministry is of ambiguous relevance. Paul had been arrested in the Temple and is eventually taken before Felix, procurator of Judea (c. 52–56 CE), to whom he explains that he had come to Jerusalem 'to bring alms to my nation and to offer sacrifices' (Acts 24.17). It is possible that this is how Paul might have discussed his collection in pagan circles. Certainly, many interpreters have understood this verse as alluding to the collection (see Downs's rejection of Luke's relevance for this topic [2008: 63-70], though he also accepts that the people named in Acts 20.4 may have belonged to Paul's collection delegation [so, e.g. Furnish 1984: 411]).

For the most part, however, we simply do not know enough about the collection effort to explain its origins or outcome more adequately. Partly, for the same reason, it is not entirely clear how Paul conceived of the collection theologically. Accordingly, Stephan Joubert quite rightly wonders whether an exclusively theological reading of the collection 'does not restrict a more holistic understanding', which would 'focu[s] on the consistent interplay on all the relevant social and theological factors' (2000: 5). In his view this means, above all, reading for the role that patronage, or, more loosely, benefaction, understood in anthropological terms as a system of social exchange, played in Paul's thinking (cf. Blanton who reads the exchange more strictly as an economy in which 'symbolic goods' can be exchanged for material goods [2001]). Joubert believes that Paul may have stuck with the collection project after Antioch for this reason. The pillars of that church had granted Paul's gospel legitimacy and, in return, were within their rights to request a service, namely the gathering of funds for the poor (2005: 6). Joubert's treatment of patronage in the earliest church is more nuanced than some in that it maps several dynamics of exchange and power at once. For instance, the original request that Antioch assist Jerusalem may have been James' attempt at establishing Jerusalem's rightful authority over one of its satellites (2005: 119). When Paul set out on his own, in addition to feeling obliged to repay

Jerusalem's favor of recognition, he might have wanted to find a way of 'secur[ing] his own ideological position over against that of Jerusalem' (2005: 125), principally by bringing great numbers of converts into the church. Then, once the collection had been delivered, there would be a reversal in the power dynamic (signaled by 2 Cor. 8.14), whereby the Jerusalem benefactors would become the Corinthians' debtors (2005: 141). And all of this develops in a religious context that deems the deity as the ultimate benefactor. Certainly, this means that Christians were in God's debt and so were obliged to offer praise and thanksgiving. But it also means that God, like any powerful human patron, gains status (2 Cor. 9.12-13) by collecting beneficiaries (2005: 147). Joubert makes the surprisingly inconsistent claim, after all this, that Jerusalem would offer prayers (9.14) on behalf of the Corinthians (and the other churches participating in the collection) not as a reciprocal obligation, but in celebration of 'the unity and equality of all believers' (2005: 148). Or perhaps the inconsistency arises from the earlier notion that Jerusalem would become Corinth's beneficiary upon receipt of the collection, for Joubert insists that such exchanges were meant for the mutual benefit of all parties. In the end, tensions among the components of his thesis—Paul's political aspirations, the instability of each party's status through a series of reciprocal exchanges, the overall impetus towards equality—may reflect nothing more than the messiness of social experience itself.

Joubert doesn't subordinate theology to social context so much as he understands the former through the latter. Something similar could be said for politically engaged readings as well, especially if 'social context' is understood as broadly as possible. Sze-Kar Wan, for example, argues that the collection 'was a daring proposal to reorder economic life together along unabashedly transcendent, universalizing [albeit from within Judaism] principles' (2000: 196; cf. Horsley 2009: 241). This is so because, as many have argued, Paul's intention (expressed perhaps in the 'sharing' or 'partnership' [*koinōnia*] of 2 Cor. 8.4 and 9.13) is, at least in part, ecumenical unity (see especially Georgi 1992). The collection makes that unity operative in Wan's view. The anti-colonial unity of the church is also, in 2 Corinthians 8–9, 'anti-patronal', partly because God is the true focus of the collection initiative, but also, intriguingly, because Paul diffuses the patronage dimension of the collection. All those involved know that they are collaborating with many others (in Macedonia, Galatia) and, thus, are aware that they cannot have exclusive claim to their human clients in Jerusalem (Wan 2000: 214; cf. Witherington who similarly sees the collection as a tool to displace the Corinthians' patronal impulses by shifting their focus from Paul to Jerusalem [1995: 342]).

Many readers begin with theology and remain more or less focused on relevant scriptural or religious contexts for interpretations. David Downs, like others, reads Paul's collection as a form of worship and the language of 2 Corinthians 8–9, especially *leitourgias* ('ministry/liturgy') in 9.12, as evidence that, for Paul, the gift to Jerusalem's poor was a 'priestly service offered to God' (2008: 145; cf. Furnish 1984: 451; Georgi 1992; 2003). The influential interpretation of Johannes Munck, which takes the function of the Gentiles in Paul's expectation for Israel, in Romans 11, as its point of departure, assumes that the collection has an eschatological significance. The donation from the Gentiles will fulfill prophecies in Mic. 4.1-2 and especially Isa. 60.5-6 concerning the pilgrimage of the nations to worship in Israel, bringing their wealth with them as tribute. Munck finds additional evidence in support of his reading in Paul's invocation of the 'hope of Israel' before Agrippa (Acts 26.6) and the 'leaders of the Jews' in Rome (Acts 28.20)—assuming, of course, that the Gentile collection offered in Jerusalem fulfilled that hope (1977: 301-305). However, few readers today find Munck's thesis compelling, despite his undeniably brilliant reliance upon Romans. Critics wonder why Paul never mentions this as the purpose of the collection, and why Paul, apparently in high eschatological mode, should, nevertheless, be planning to visit Rome after a stay in Jerusalem on his way to further and future mission fields in Spain (Rom. 15.28; e.g. Harris 2005: 99; Thrall 2000: 513).

There are other systematic approaches to the theology of the collection, of course, but it may be most helpful to restrict our discussion to a few key passages in 2 Corinthians 8–9 that are examined theologically by most readers. The first, or the first cluster of verses really, is those in which Paul uses 'grace' to describe not only divine benevolence (8.1, 9; 9.15), but also the collection itself. The Macedonians request the 'privilege [*charin*] of sharing in this ministry' (8.4) and the collection is a 'generous undertaking/ act [*charin*]' (8.6, 7, 19). Most readers would prefer to distinguish strictly between a 'non-theological' grace in acts of human agency and divine grace. But this is a problem for Kathy Ehrensperger, who wonders instead what this grace could mean outside of the spiritualizing tendency of theological reception. In her view, similar to that of Sze-Kar Wan, just mentioned, grace refers to 'a network of horizontal solidarity among all Christ-followers' (2009: 79). It is 'the doing of justice' (2009: 76), in a 'network of open mutuality' (2009: 69). Which is not to say that it is not connected to a divine source, however. Even for readers who consider human grace in quite ordinary, apolitical terms, grace in our text is discerned as a spiritual gift, akin to speaking in tongues, say, in acts of human generosity. The collection can, thus, be seen as an initiative enabled, especially miraculously in the case of the very poor Macedonians, by God's own giving spirit (Downs 2008: 132; Thrall 2000: 594; Gaventa 1999: 54; Barrett 1973: 220, 222). Dieter Georgi extends the discussion of the collection as grace into Paul's idea of the 'fair balance' in 2 Cor. 8.13-14. If Paul and other Hellenistic writers, such as Philo, conceived

of this 'equity' as a cosmic (wisdom/gnostic) principle, then the willing-
ness to participate in the collection is evidence that 'what moves the inner
person also forms the universe, and vice-versa' (Georgi 1992: 89). Joubert,
like others (see Thrall 2000: 540), disagrees with Georgi's reading, but still
sees value in thinking that Paul intentionally builds upon the word's 'positive connotations of harmony, peace and justice' (2000: 141). Important in
this discussion is the 'generous act of our Lord Jesus Christ, that though he
was rich, yet for your sakes became poor' (2 Cor. 8.9). Most commentators
understand the verse as evidence of Paul's pre-existence Christology (e.g.
Harris: 2005: 579; Thrall 2000: 534; Barrett 1973: 223), although some
limit the concept of grace here to Christ's incarnation and passion (so Dunn
1998: 292; Furnish 1984: 417). Joerg Rieger understands the parallel with
the hymn in Phil. 2.6-8 also to mean that, in 2 Corinthians, Paul was using
the collection to convince his recipients 'to practice kenosis in the community' (2007: 51; cf. Horrell 1996: 232; but see Joubert who does not think
Paul is setting Christ forth as a model [2000: 179]).

One of Paul's scriptural citations in 2 Corinthians 9 carries a certain
ambiguous theological significance, too. The LXX version of Ps. 112.9,
quoted in 2 Cor. 9.9, identifies the pious person as the one who 'scatters
abroad' and 'gives to the poor'. Although Paul undoubtedly knew this, he,
nevertheless, implies in context that the scatterer is God, for 9.8 constructs
a parallel image—'God is able to provide you with every blessing'—making
God, not the pious person, and, thus by extension, not the generous
Corinthian either, the immediate referent of 'he' in 9.9. Betz claims that
Paul's agrarian theological imagery in 9.6-14 is not specifically Christian,
but is simply borrowed from the broader culture and 'reflect[s] ... the common religious sentiment of antiquity' (1985: 113). Be that as it may, readers
have puzzled over whether or not to understand the subject in divine (e.g.
Barnett 1997: 440) or human (e.g. Thrall 2000: 583) terms. The meaning of 'righteousness' in 9.9b obviously hangs on the determination of the
verse's subject. If it is God who scatters, then God's righteousness, God's
covenant fidelity, 'endures forever'. But, if the farm hand here is really the
Corinthian donor, then his or her righteousness is a 'generosity to the poor
[that] will remain a way of life' (Harris 2005: 641). Frequently referred to
in studies of this verse is Dieter Georgi's elegant idea that both readings are
perhaps simultaneously viable. Paul deploys a 'deliberate vagueness' which
'necessarily leads one to realize that God is the true origin of human com-
passion and that [God's] righteousness is the true source of our righteousness' (1992: 99).

6

Moses' Veil in Post-Pauline Reception

That mysterious emblem was never once withdrawn. It shook with his measured breath as he gave out the psalm; it threw its obscurity between him and the holy page, as he read the Scriptures; and while he prayed, the veil lay heavily on his uplifted countenance. Did he seek to hide it from the dread Being whom he was addressing?

—Nathaniel Hawthorne, 'The Minister's Black Veil'

The title of this final chapter promises far more than the chapter itself can deliver, for an adequate reception study of 2 Corinthians 3 would require a space more expansive than this. Nevertheless, I would like to close this short book with a gesture towards the reception study of a New Testament text because reception, variously defined, is an increasingly important mode of biblical studies scholarship. Reception study brings Paul, in this case, into conversation with later texts in order to challenge a consensus reading or to highlight the historical- and cultural-groundedness of specific interpretations. It can also, more traditionally, trace a history of readings with the aim of illustrating the enduring, if protean, significance of a biblical text over time. In some cases, reception study might do all of the above, and more (for a representative sampling of reception approaches, see the recent *Oxford Handbook of the Reception History of The Bible* [Lieb *et al.* 2011]). My aim, informed by the work of scholars such as Erin Runions, Mieke Bal, Yvonne Sherwood, Roland Boer and others, will be to rethink Paul (or a reading of Paul) through a subsequent cultural text, or texts, specifically so that the Christian supersessionism so common in interpretations of 2 Corinthians 3 might be re-contextualized and, I hope, challenged.

Lutheran Readings

The typical understanding of this passage concludes that Jewish readers of the 'old covenant' (3.14), or of Moses as a metonym for the old covenant (3.15), fail to understand the true spiritual meaning of scripture. Like Moses in Exod. 34.33-35, the Jewish reader reads as though behind a veil (2 Cor. 3.15); or like Pharaoh, from whom Israel had escaped, they read with a 'hardened' mind (3.14). It is only 'when one turns to the Lord [that] the veil is removed' (3.16)—that is, when one embraces Christ, through conversion perhaps, but certainly in opposition to those who do not live in the 'freedom' of the 'spirit of the Lord' (3.17), but 'practice cunning [and] ... falsify God's word' (4.2). For Paul, apparently, the Jews as Jews, as an interpretive community (or communities), engaged in scriptural reflection as part of a multiform and complex religious life, were 'blinded' and in darkness to the light of Christ (4.4, 6). As Barrett puts it, 'that which was being abolished ... [was] the old covenant, or dispensation, as a whole, the religious framework under which Israel was constituted as a people' (1973: 119).

Individual versions of this reading may vary, but they have a very long history. In 1521, Martin Luther defended himself against a critic by means of a sophisticated explanation of the 'letter' (3.3, 6) and the literal meaning of scripture, essentially denying the primary validity of church-sanctioned (i.e. allegorical or typological) interpretations. The problem, Luther realized, in typically charming polemical fashion, was that the letter/Spirit dichotomy, and even anything in this text referring to the Spirit itself, is always already 'letter'. It thus cannot be the case that the literal meaning of a text kills, for, if that were true, then embracing the literal sense of 'the Spirit gives life' would, paradoxically, kill. Or, to put it differently, a spiritual reading of Moses, like Paul's here, or of any other figure or event mentioned in the Hebrew Bible, becomes 'a new literal sense', a new letter to be read plainly from the text of the New Testament (2005: 78). The difference with which Paul is concerned in 2 Corinthians 3, Luther argues, is the difference between ministries. 'Paul does not write one iota' in this passage about allegorical versus literal meanings, but 'only about two kinds of preaching' (2005: 80). Those two kinds are represented by the Old Testament and the New, or more directly by Catholicism and a reform movement such as his. Most importantly, Luther combats here a reading that fails to recognize that 'the letter kills' because the purpose of the Law is to show us that we are as good as dead in our sins without the grace of Christ (2005: 82). Behind it all, however, is the more fundamental binary Jew/Christian, according to which the Jews are rhetorically aligned with condemnation, misery, murder (2005: 83).

Although this is not necessarily the best example of a 'Lutheran' reading of Paul, much New Perspective scholarship argues that Luther's interpretations—on central matters like justification by faith, for instance—were frequently entirely wrong (see the 'Whimsical Introduction' to Stephen Westerholm's *Perspectives Old and New on Paul: The 'Lutheran' Paul and his Critics* [2004], which imagines the stunned response of Luther *redivivus*). With regard to 2 Corinthians 3 in particular, one might argue that the 'Lutheran' reading of Paul is wrong because Paul was not in any way

claiming the end, the obsolescence of the old covenant (3.13). And yet a
reader as decidedly un-Lutheran, in this sense, as Daniel Boyarin can argue
forcefully that Paul's own 'supersessionism cannot be denied' (1994: 104; cf.
Stockhausen 1989: 167). Oddly, in some ways Boyarin's reading does parallel Luther's, for both understand Paul's terms ('letter', 'spirit') as internal to
a single hermeneutic, rather than referring to two different modes of reading (1994: 86). Boyarin indicates that Paul is troubling for Jewish readers,
certainly, but that in 'the first century, the contest between a Pauline allegorical Israel and a rabbinic hermeneutics of the concrete Israel is simply a
legitimate cultural, hermeneutical and political contestation' (1994: 105).
Luther, of course, is less capable of such contextualizing nuance and, at
any rate, the hermeneutical issue is clearly subordinate in his mind to the
ideological one, according to which pope, priest, 'sophist' (i.e. scholastic
theologians [2005: 83]), Torah and Jew are displaced by a specific understanding of spirit and grace.

Most modern readers make a point of illustrating the logic of 2 Cor.
3.7-11, sometimes in order to forestall supersessionist interpretations. It is
evident that Paul grants tremendous significance to that which was now
'set aside' (3.7). The 'ministry of death' (3.7), the 'ministry of condemnation' (3.9), like the 'ministry of the Spirit' (3.8) and the 'ministry of justification' (3.9), 'came in glory' (3.7; cf. 3.9, 10, 11), even if the earlier glory
has been surpassed by a 'greater glory' (3.10). Using a rabbinical interpretive device known as *qal wahomer*, or 'from the lesser to the greater', Paul
contrasts the glory of each, but does not deny that Moses' ministry was a
glorious ministry. If anything, the ministry of the Spirit is an intensifica-
tion of the Mosaic glory. So there is continuity. And yet that Mosaic glory
is also lesser. The term Paul uses in 3.7, 11, 13 and 14 to specify what
has become of the lesser glory derives from the verb often translated into
English as 'fade', 'pass away' or 'be set aside'. Readers point out, however,
that the verb usually suggests nullification, invalidation, a state of inop-
erability, and, thus, that Paul is saying, in 3.7, that the glory shining on
Moses' face 'was being annulled' (Furnish 1984: 201; but see Harris who
prefers 'faded away' [2005: 280]). It is also noted that the idea that Moses'
glory faded, or was being abolished, may be Paul's invention. The narrative
in Exod. 34.29-36, in fact, implies just the opposite; Moses' face always
shone. The veil is meant to allay the fears of the Israelites, who found it
difficult to bear Moses' splendor (Exod. 34.30). When speaking with the
Lord and when communicating a commandment to the people, Moses
would remove the veil, but he wore it at all other times, it seems (Exod.
34.33, 35). Nowhere in the text is there the slightest hint that Moses
donned the veil to hide his dying light, although Margaret Thrall allows
that the idea could be 'implicit' in the text, but 'only for those determined

to see some disparaging element in it' (1994: 243). Would this include Paul? For others (e.g. Harris 2005: 285, drawing upon Childs 1995: 621) 'it is natural to deduce' that Moses' glory was frequently in need of 'recharging'. Commentators regularly provide evidence that early Jewish readers took the text to mean that the glory was permanent (but, again, Harris thinks he has found a potential first-century source for Paul's thinking in Pseudo-Philo [2005: 285]). Whether or not he is fully an exegetical innovator in his reading, Paul uses the Exodus text to create contrasts between Moses and himself and between Jewish readers of scriptures and believers in Christ. Or possibly 'contrasts' isn't exactly correct since Christians 'with unveiled faces [see] the glory of the Lord ... [and] are being transformed ... from one degree of glory to another' (3.18). There is some debate about who the Lord is, Christ (e.g. Barrett 1973: 125) or God (e.g. Thrall 1994: 283), but, regardless, Moses seems to be the model of the unveiled believer, for he too was unveiled when in the presence of the divine. On the other hand, if the glory were fading and Moses donned his veil from a lack of boldness (cf. Paul's own claims to boldness in 2 Cor. 3.12; 7.4; 10.1-2) and in order to keep Israel ignorant of the end of that glory (3.13), then it may be possible to accuse him of a certain kind of deceit (Given 2001: 123; cf. Furnish who disallows this reading [1984: 232-33]).

Paul's reason for turning to an exegesis of Exodus 34 at this point is not very clear. Joseph Fitzmyer proposes that Paul simply free-associates, moving from letters of recommendation in 3.1 to letters on the heart in 3.2 (citing Jer. 31.33, or perhaps Ezek. 11.19 or 36.26), ultimately to the stone tablets of 3.3 (alluding to Exod. 34.1), and so on (1993: 69-70; but Murphy-O'Connor objects that such a reading makes Paul seem excessively 'mercurial' [2010: 31]). Most readers assume that Paul is here responding to an interest in Moses on the part of his critics and that there is a polemical dimension to his exegesis. Paul Duff advances an intriguing variant of this reading, but one which, importantly, challenges the traditional supersessionist paradigm. Paul may be responding to critics, but their criticism pertained to Gentiles, who live under, but are disobedient to, Jewish law. Citing a variety of ancient texts which held, in effect, that the whole world had access to the Torah, but only Israel obeyed it (cf. Rom. 1.18-23), Duff suggests that 'the ministry of condemnation' refers to the condemnation specifically of Gentiles (2004: 326). The veil over Israel's mind now means only that Israel has not yet understood that God's position vis-à-vis the Gentiles has altered (2004: 328). For whatever reason, some in Corinth worried about their exclusion from the covenant; perhaps, as a result, they were inclined to participate more fully in the letter of the law. Paul's purpose in this text is to reassure them that in Christ their condemnation has been annulled (3.14).

One of the most significant recent studies attempting to read 2 Corinthians 3 against the traditional Lutheran grain is that of Scott Hafemann. His study, *Paul, Moses, and the History of Israel*, begins by indicating that the Pauline consonance with tradition links Paul directly to Moses, both of whom were inadequate for their ministry—partly, in each case, because of their weakness as speakers—but were made adequate by God (2 Cor. 2.16; 3.5-6; 1996: 40-41, 107). The apparent contrast between Moses and Paul is thereby called into question. As is any real difference between Israel and those in Christ, for Hafemann places the entire passage into a Jewish eschatological context. Reading the intertextual links with Jeremiah (31.31-33) and Ezekiel (11.19; 36.26), among other relevant passages, in the context of post-biblical Jewish interpretation, Hafemann argues that Paul 'picks up the common theme ... of "the nation's 'hard heart,'" while at the same time expressing hope in God's corresponding eschatological promise to replace the 'heart of stone' with a *new* heart of flesh and a new spirit/Holy Spirit so that his people might keep the law and thus remain faithful to the covenant"' (1996: 140, citing Hafemann 1986: 213). The letter kills only because of persistent disobedience, exemplified most powerfully by the golden calf episode of Exodus 32 (1996: 377). Remember that the passage Paul cites, from Exodus 34, is the *second* giving of the law. Moses' veil in that story, according to Hafemann, is a merciful protection from divine wrath—God's glory was also God's judgment upon his people (1996: 359). In fact, 'the end of the glory', in Hafemann's understanding is taken teleologically as punishment, destruction. That is, the aim of the law was the condemnation of Israel's disobedience (1996: 358). The veil is, thus, both the renewal of the covenant and the suspension of its punitive function, which was 'set aside', or as Hafemann has it, 'rendered inoperative' despite the continuing hardness of Israel's hearts and minds (1996: 311). Now, however, in Paul's 'eschatological, restoration interpretation' of Exodus 34, true obedience has become possible in Christ (1996: 393), who brings freedom from the hard-heartedness that had plagued the covenantal bond (1996: 405). It is as though Christians, the obedient, 'spirit-filled remnant' (cf. Rom. 11.5; 1996: 454)—be they Jewish or Gentile—now have the eschatological opportunity to return with him, as with Moses, to Sinai again (1996: 138, 455).

Hafemann's work has been criticized because it tries to suggest an equivalence between the old and the new covenant (Meyer 2009: 112; Kim 2002: 158), even though this seems precisely the value of its conclusions. A more pertinent complaint is that this sort of project relies far too heavily on understandings of canon and literary context that may not have been Paul's own, and/or that very likely would have been entirely lost on his audience (DiMattei 2008: 87; cf. Stanley 2008; Given [2001: 119] essentially calls Hafemann's project a 'disaster' in this regard). Not only is there the potential for inaccuracy, or interpretive overreach, but something of Paul's own personality, an element of his idiosyncratic style, might also be lost in the search for determinative scriptural or literary sources and parallels. Richard Hays cautions us to be attentive to Paul's 'helter-skelter intuitive readings, [to their] unpredictable, ungeneralizable' character (1993: 160).

Paul's Black Veil

Literary theorist J. Hillis Miller says more or less the same thing: 'The veil is the type and symbol of the fact that all signs are potentially unreadable, or that the reading of them is potentially unverifiable' (1991: 97). Although Miller is writing about the veil in Nathaniel Hawthorne's short story 'The Minister's Black Veil', rather than Moses' veil in 2 Corinthians 3, his critical reading is apropos for our reading of Paul in the context of Paul's reading of Moses. For Paul himself, the apostle admits, after exegetically unmasking Moses as a faulty type of his own ministry, also wears a veil. Or almost. 'Our gospel is veiled', he admits in 2 Cor. 4.3, 'it is veiled to those who are perishing.' Perhaps the very reason Paul performs the exegesis of Exodus 34 in the first place is because he has been accused of some obscurity himself (Furnish 1984: 247; Barrett 1973: 130), or lack of rhetorical skill (Murphy-O'Connor 2010: 143), or ineffectiveness in ministering to his own fellow Jews (Thrall 1994: 304); or it is because of his active suppression of wisdom and women's spiritual agency (as in 1 Cor. 11.3f; Theissen 1987: 126), or his intentional, if initial, misrepresentation of his message to the 'weak' Gentiles, or to Jews he hopes to reach (Given 2001: 117); or, finally, it may be that he is appropriating a more positive understanding of the veil from among those who read Exodus 34 as an indication of special status (Georgi 1986: 261-62). However one understands 2 Cor. 4.3, the doubling of the veil can be a serious problem if Moses' unveiling before the Lord is taken as emblematic of Christian conversion or community. Just when the veil is lifted, just when 'all of us, with unveiled faces, [see] the glory of the Lord' in our own radiant transformation (2 Cor. 3.18), just then we encounter Paul, veiled, and experience what Miller aptly calls 'the preternatural horror of unveiling the possibility of the impossibility of unveiling' (1991: 75).

Paul's veil, or Paul's veiled reading of Moses' veil, is sometimes taken to be an indirect inspiration for Hawthorne's story (Dunne 2010: 87; Britt 2004: 90), even if Hawthorne's interpreters frequently turn to other New Testament passages instead, including 1 Cor. 11.3-15; 13.12; 2 Cor. 5.16; 11.2 (depending upon the story detail requiring illumination). Revelation is also among the texts mentioned, insofar as the tale holds out, but always defers, the promise of unveiling. Published in 1836, 'The Minister's Black

Veil' tells the story of Parson Hooper of Milford, Connecticut who appears, one fine Sunday morning, wearing a veil of black crape. He preaches that first day on a 'subject [that] had reference to secret sin, and those sad mysteries which we hide from our nearest and dearest, and would fain conceal from our own consciousnesses, even forgetting that the Omniscient can detect them' (1987: 187-88). Later the same day, he conducts the funeral service for a young woman and celebrates at the marriage of a young couple, all the while hiding his face, except his mouth—which bore 'a sad smile ... like a faint glimmering of light' (1987: 194)—behind his black veil. What had been a happy community soon falls into anxious dread whenever Mr Hooper passes by or performs his ministerial duties. Hooper sometimes even shocks himself if he chances to glance unsuspectingly in a mirror or pool. The delegation of townspeople sent to reason with him finds itself 'speechless, confused, and shrinking uneasily from Mr Hooper's eye, which they felt to be fixed upon them with an invisible glance' (1987: 192). They leave without so much as raising the topic. His betrothed, Elizabeth, has more courage. She asks him to remove the veil, but he responds that he cannot, for he has taken a vow of some kind. He comments, further, that 'this veil is a type and a symbol' (1987: 193), but of what he doesn't say. Does he harbor sorrow? Sin? Possibly, but he is no different from any other person in that regard. Still, he will not remove it, not until all souls are unveiled in the next world. For Elizabeth, this is tragically unacceptable. She leaves and they never marry. Hooper 'smile[s] to think that only a material emblem had separated him from his happiness, though the horrors which it shadowed forth, must be drawn darkly between the fondest of lovers' (1987: 195). Eventually, known as Father Hooper, the parson grows old in the course of time and nears his end. But even then he refuses to unveil his face. Despite his weakened state, he engages those around him (including the aged, and faithfully single, Elizabeth) with a surprising vigor. 'Why do you tremble at me alone?' he asks:

> 'Tremble also at each other! Have men avoided me, and women shown no pity, and children screamed and fled, only for my black veil? What, but the mystery which it obscurely typifies, has made this piece of crape so awful? When the friend shows his inmost heart to his friend; the lover to his best-beloved; when man does not shrink vainly from the eye of his Creator, loathsomely treasuring up the secret of his sin; then deem me a monster, for the symbol beneath which I have lived and die! I look around me, and, lo! on every visage a Black Veil!' (1987: 199).

Upon which he falls to his pillow 'a veiled corpse' and is buried in the grave, his face eternally darkened by the black crape (1987: 199).

Since the story's publication, readers (like Milford's fictional townsfolk) have wondered about the mystery typified by Hooper's veil. Edgar Allan

Poe suggested 'that a crime of dark dye, (having reference to the 'young lady') [had] been committed' (quoted in Person 2007: 48). Although it is unclear which young lady he means, in all likelihood she would be the deceased woman whose corpse is said (by a number of unreliable witnesses) to have 'shuddered' when Mr Hooper accidentally revealed his face as he bowed over the casket and who accompanied him along the road to the burial ground and, who, finally, reappeared at the wedding as a ghostly proxy for the bride (Hawthorne 1987: 189-91). But no real crime need be posited. Most of Mr Hooper's contemporaries would probably have agreed with the Reverend Mr Clark of Westbury who, having come to attend upon his elder's passing, declared Parson Hooper 'a man ... given to prayer, of ... blameless example, holy in deed and thought, so far as mortal judgment may pronounce' (1987: 198). The fact is that Hawthorne simply gives us no terribly useful clues for unveiling Mr Hooper's mystery. Many scholars of American literature, Michael Colacurcio foremost among them, argue that Hawthorne's fascination with his Puritan cultural heritage requires us to seek answers in history. Accordingly, Mr Hooper can be seen as an awakened eighteenth-century peer of a figure like Jonathan Edwards, who could also scare the daylights out of congregants despite his (similarly) mild nature (Colacurcio 1995: 323). Hooper would, thus, be symbolizing the true nature of sin, of innate human depravity, with his veil. But, like other of Hawthorne's extreme characters, Hooper, whose 'conscious decision has been everywhere to signify the absolute rather than to embody the relative' (Colacurcio 1995: 349), fails to achieve much more than an ineffectual isolation. He never awakens his congregation to his own insight because he refuses to compromise that insight through language, teaching, conversation. Actually, Hawthorne calls Hooper 'a very efficient clergyman', but only because the parson's veil 'enabled him to sympathize with all dark affections' (1987: 196). Or that is how it seemed to souls in dire straits, those who would call upon Parson Hooper in their times of trial. As for the ordinary folk of Milford, week in and week out, Hooper was little more than a 'Fool for Truth' (Colacurcio 1995: 345), albeit a Truth they could not understand.

There are other historical contexts to consider, including Hawthorne's contemporary social world, in which abolitionists were lighting the fires that would become the American Civil War. John Birk's 'Hawthorne's Mister Hooper: The Veil of Ham?' (1996) traces echoes of William Lloyd Garrison's oratory and journalism in Hawthorne's tale, while also considering Hooper's black visage, and especially the response to it, as a highly mediated reflection upon the treatment of African Americans.

Like J. Hillis Miller's influential deconstructionist reading, this scholarship helps to bring Hawthorne's tale into conversation with Paul and readings of

Paul. And there are some interesting similarities. For instance, Birk's essay calls to mind Brad Braxton's reading of the veil in 2 Corinthians 3 in terms of 'veil' language in W.E.B. Du Bois's *The Souls of Black Folk*. Du Bois considered the veil a psychological barrier to self-understanding among African Americans, a perspective on identity warped by white racism (Braxton 2008: 422). Assuming that Paul genuinely represents an ideal of reconciliation in 2 Cor. 5.19, Braxton wonders how we can read him in the effort to heal, through various kinds of reparations, the wounds caused by the trans-Atlantic slave trade. But the question is complicated by a number of factors: that colonial slavers were obviously Christian and could rely upon slavery language in the New Testament; that Paul's choice of Exodus 34 implicates the 'greater glory' of Christianity in a covenant renewal that came 'at the expense of indigenous people' (Braxton 2008: 421); and, that 'in some sense, Paul does to Judaism what later Christian missionaries did to African Traditional Religion—deny its enduring validity' (Braxton 2008: 426). This requires us to read Christian supersessionism as racism and perhaps not only in contexts like the African missionary field, where such intersectional analysis is necessary. Working along these lines, we might reverse Birk's thesis and say that Mr Hooper, likewise, conflates race with primordial sin. His black veil prevents others from seeing most of his expressions and his hidden eyes especially disconcert his congregation. But he is, nevertheless, always said to smile in a way that glimmers like light (Hawthorne 1987: 189, 192-94, 199). Indeed, Elizabeth asks him to remove the veil and thus to 'let the sun shine from behind the cloud' (1987: 193). Mr Hooper's face is a white, shining face. A face like Moses' or like that of the Christian in 2 Cor. 3.18. The veil produces isolation for the parson not because it marks him with blackness, but more likely because it projects blackness, because it brings him to see his parishioners as racially other ('lo! on every visage a Black Veil!'), and monstrously so. If Hooper were more self-consciously Pauline, he might even have railed against the monstrously blinded minds and darkened faces of 'the perishing' around him who cannot see that his glimmering light is 'the glory of Christ ... the image of God' (2 Cor. 4.4). Colacurcio accuses Mr Hooper of assuming for himself the divine vision 'of the Calvinist God' (1995: 325), so this extrapolation from the tale is not entirely improbable. Hooper's projection of darkness is also incredibly ironic. He is like the Paul who declares that he has 'renounced the shameful things that one hides' (2 Cor. 4.2) just before acknowledging his own hiding veil. After all, is not Hooper precisely the kind of individual he rails against, the 'friend' and 'lover' who refuses to show 'his inmost heart' to friend and 'best-beloved'?

Questions of race and ethnicity need to be contextualized carefully in studies of Paul, of course. In a reception study, however, Paul himself is less consequential than significant readings of Paul and their socio-cultural implications. Juxtaposing Mr Hooper with a Paul considered in the light of Du Bois, racism and postcolonial struggle, not to mention the ideological conflicts between pro-slavery ministers and abolitionists in advance of the Civil War, enables a more historically-specific reception reading. For instance, as J. Albert Harrill notes, abolitionists, during the period in which Hawthorne wrote 'The Minister's Black Veil', found it difficult to understand the New Testament conflict between the egalitarianism of the gospel and Paul's slavery-tolerant household codes. Some concluded that, for the sake of expediency, Paul's anti-slavery perspectives had to be expressed in careful, even coded terms, so as not to bring the wrath of Rome down on the early church. Such an anxiety was probably more reflective of US anti-slavery moderates and conservatives, perhaps, than of Paul. William Ellery Channing, for example, in his *Slavery* (1836), argues strenuously against pro-slavery scriptural justifications, but he also cautions that Paul was less than fully clear on the topic because to advocate 'servile war' would have 'shaken the social fabric to its foundation' (Channing 1836: 122; Harrill 2006: 173). Perhaps an even more intriguing intertext is Olaudah Equiano's *Interesting Narrative*. This autobiography of a self-emancipated slave, originally published in the late eighteenth century, was reprinted extensively, including by New York and Boston houses, into the 1830s (Potkay 1995: 163). Equiano writes that the veil of Isa. 25.7 (KJV), which 'is spread over all nations', was removed from his mind as he contemplated scriptures, and specifically Acts 4.12: 'the Lord was pleased to break in upon my soul with his bright beams of heavenly light' (2003: 190). Vincent Wimbush argues that, in the narration of his conversion moment, Equiano's 'rhetorical strategy ... signal[ed] to the reader the mysterious truth about the inclusion of black peoples in God's family and, even more difficult to fathom, the truth about the black person as the figure of divine presence in the world' (Wimbush 2012: 147). Although it might take us too far afield to recall how such language echoes Paul Duff's reading of 2 Corinthians 3, cited above, regarding the inclusion of Gentiles, all of the sources under discussion here support the viability of Birk's claims about Hawthorne's motives.

Reading 2 Corinthians 3 alongside 'The Minister's Black Veil' might challenge us to recast Paul's potentially supersessionist logic, and, more importantly, the cultural politics of exclusion evident at 2 Cor. 4.3, in terms of racial bigotry, that is, in ways the majority of readers of Paul would find objectionable. Paul, like Mr Hooper, is a genuine voice of Christian freedom who, nevertheless, dooms (to a perishing obscurity) those whom he exiles to the margins of, or because of, his gospel. And those critics or opponents (or unenlightened friends) are doomed by means of the very device—the veil, the gospel, the Christian scriptures preached by pro-slavery pastors and moderate/conservative abolitionists alike—that Paul, like Mr Hooper, adapts for the sake of others' freedom. This is not to conflate texts and contexts in any simplistic way, but rather to suggest, through an interpretive contiguity, the dangers lurking in a passage the history of which should give more pause to readers than it does. Luther's anti-Jewish Paul is still our Paul, unless we can experience him differently, perhaps by shifting focus temporarily, and changing, if only for a moment, the terms of the debate.

Considering race in America in the 1830s is historically important to a reading of the Pauline traces in Mr Hooper's veil. But one can extend the same logic more generally to contemporary situations, as D.A. Miller does in his (deconstructive) reading of J. Hillis Miller's deconstructive reading of the Hawthorne story. The specifics of this curious debate between two critical schools is perhaps less significant for our purposes than D.A. Miller's accusation that J. Hillis Miller's deconstruction, at least in this case, replicates Hooper's authoritatively, impersonally maintained controlling gesture:

> The minister's black veil ... serves as an emblem of the professional deformation that positively requires ... alienation for efficient job performance—and not just, of course, from those who aren't white, male, or heterosexual-identified but also (even more, of course) from those who, like Hooper, are so entitled.
>
> The veil parabolically alludes to the power Hooper derives from ascetically renouncing his own psychological determinations in favor of a rigorous identification with a totalizing structure that interprets them, but only at the price of despecifying them (1987: 52).

Earlier in this section, I alluded to J. Hillis Miller's much-quoted notion that the veil is essentially a sign of the impossibility of interpretation. In D.A. Miller's view, the veil is rather an administrative function, one which prevents communion precisely because it requires a universalizing evacuation of the personal on the part of the administrator. Mr Hooper becomes Father Hooper to the extent the man a community affectionately used to see as 'our parson' adopts the blinding perspective of 'no mortal eye', and so ends his life a 'dark old man', obscurely generic and unknowable (Hawthorne 1987: 185, 193, 199). A reading, such as that of J. Hillis Miller, that celebrates this very obscurity, is a reading that implicitly endorses dehumanizing structures of power. The parson's veil is text, D.A. Miller says, only when it is no longer 'texture' (Miller 1987: 52). Or, in the words of William Ellery Channing, social fabric.

Paul's personality is so vivid, his voice so personal in its intensity, that it may be hard to understand the relevance of D.A. Miller's critical language to a study of 2 Corinthians 3. But recall Graham Shaw's charges in *The Cost of Authority* that, in addition to the imperialism of universality, Paul's message involves 'a view of other men which subordinates all ordinary human distinctions to the new Christian identity' (1983: 115). Shaw is thinking of 2 Cor. 5.15 and 17 in particular. He goes on, more critically, to allege that Paul's reliance upon a divine model for his ministry essentially creates a two-tier identity system that disadvantages the Corinthians themselves, whose personalities suffer a 'radical displacement' (1983: 114). Paul 'gains identity by submitting to a Christ who is largely the creation of his own projections. The believer can only achieve a divine identity by surrendering to Christ's apostle, who is no projection, but has a will and a determination of his own' (Shaw 1983: 115). Now, many readers will and do find Shaw's approach problematic, as we noted above in Chapter 4. Also, D.A. Miller's complaint about Mr Hooper's veil implies something quite different from what Shaw describes here. Hooper empties *himself* of identity and therein lies his strange power. But Shaw's understanding of identity displacement is, I would argue, implicit in Miller's reading of the Hawthorne story. Mr Hooper, representing humanity as abstraction, means to represent his parishioners also in terms of that abstraction. Indeed, at the end of the story, he essentially projects his veil onto everybody, defacing the community as much as himself. Analogously, we note how a contemporary philosopher like Alain Badiou can take Paul's conversion as paradigmatic of political subject formation itself. The subject, after such a change, finds that his or her 'identitarian and communitarian categories' are 'absented' from the (in this case) political being of the new creation (2003: 11). For Badiou, this is why there is no longer Greek nor Jew, because prior measures of identification simply fall away, or no longer have any significance. Whether or not Paul ever really thought in these terms, it is certainly the case that readers have not hesitated to posit the Pauline text's power to absent, in this sense. Ron Cameron and Merrill Miller even advocate referring only to 'some Corinthians' in scholarship on the Corinthian correspondence as a way of avoiding this problem. In their view, the use of 'the Corinthians' might do justice to Paul's own address, but it also 'sets limits in advance on the range and scope of differences between Paul's rhetorical aims and behavioral ideals, between his convictions about his own identity and authority, and Corinthian practices, identities and recognition of authority' (2011: 245-46).

When it comes to the veil in Paul, one can see fairly easily how the question of identity can play out, sometimes in powerfully disturbing ways. As Victor Furnish puts it, with breathtaking historical insensitivity, 'God's people' are no longer futilely involved in something 'whose destiny is *extinction*', namely, whatever it is that Moses' veil hides (the law, yes, but also Judaism?), and now belong to eternity (Furnish 1984: 242; emphasis mine). The eternal, universal identity of the Christian is characterized here by, above all else, its non-coincidence with any Jewish specificity, which is, in this formulation, fated to fade away. Or go extinct, as it were. In a 'Lutheran' reading resonating more fully with the passage from Miller's essay, quoted above, David Fredrickson argues that Moses' veil is an emblem of shame and that when the veil is removed, in 2 Cor. 3.16, shame gives way to freedom, because 'freedom [is] dependant on a good conscience' (1998: 119). It follows that, if the freedom of the good conscience is Christian, then the shame of bad faith must be Jewish. Again, as seems so frequently to be the case, identity and authority, in readings of Paul's letters and the exegetical, ideological and rhetorical justifications they rely upon, seem to return to the basic problem of Christian supersessionism. But Fredrickson also goes on, still in a historical mode, but with clear contemporary significance, to claim that 'the shame that in the Greco-Roman world was attached to being poor, female and slave is removed by the Spirit' (1998: 119). This, I should emphasize, is not an exegesis of Gal. 3.28, but rather of 2 Corinthians 3, which can only mean that Moses' shame, the shame entailed in the old covenant itself, is somehow like the shame of poverty, women and the enslaved or oppressed, as well the shame of foreign birth and youth (1998: 116). Fredrickson's essay argues for the 'extreme democracy' (1998: 117) of Paul's communities and, one assumes, of the potential for radical egalitarianism in the contemporary church, a church in which adherence to an authority is less important than 'transformation to an image' (2 Cor. 3.18; Fredrickson 1998: 119). All of this is to the good. The problem lies in the exegetical linkages. In 2 Corinthians 3, it is the law, or Moses' glory, or a Jewish way of reading, that is coming to an end, and not (just) the shame of the law, or Moses, or Jewish hermeneutics; does this mean, for those variously disempowered and marginalized, that their 'shame' will likewise come to an end only when or insofar as they cease to be or think as women, slaves, foreigners, children? There is something Rawlsian about this vision of the church's democratic space; one must bracket one's primary identifications in order to participate in the public sphere (Rawls 1971). In theory, or ideally, that might also mean that not only Judaism, but also white male heterosexuality is bracketed. But white male heterosexuality has a way of taking itself as the unmarked norm of subject formation, and is necessarily re-introduced as the neutral ground of democratic debate (see Mills 2007: 110, on the unacknowledged whiteness at the heart of John Rawls' work), while Judaism, say, or lesbianism, is not. The lesson of Mr Hooper's veil for Pauline studies, then, is a lesson of what happens to identity given a certain understanding of authority. Even if specific identities are acknowledged (the glory of Moses' face), they are, nevertheless, to be subsumed, 'set aside' (2 Cor. 3.7, 11, 13-14), 'permanent[ly]' (2 Cor. 3.11), under the new regime. As caught up as we might be by Paul's language of transformation from glory to glory, we need to ask: if such glory comes at the cost of excising specificities of all kinds, is it really worth it?

But there is another, more positive way of reading the veil. Mr Hooper's veil is sometimes recognized as a form of transvestism (e.g. by both Millers; see also Stouck and Giltrow 1997: 565), because a 'lady', early in the story, remarks, '[H]ow strange ... that a simple black veil, such as any woman might wear on her bonnet, should become such a terrible thing on Mr Hooper's face' (Hawthorne 1987: 189). It seems true that, even in usurping gender ambiguity for himself, Mr Hooper effectively converts it into a powerful certainty by becoming the Father. Still, if anything goes extinct, or is absented in 'The Minister's Black Veil', it is Hooper himself. He might become an effective authority, in some circumstances, but mostly he becomes a nullity, a void like the grave into which he and his veil are consigned at the story's end. The veil, on the other hand, as an ambiguity of gender that renders him terrible in certain eyes, remains. As, of course, does Paul's own. Fredrickson refers, intriguingly, to 'the unveiled Moses and the unveiled Paul' as models of a church without shame (1998: 119), while failing to recognize that, in 2 Cor. 4.3, Paul is re-veiled. If the veil is shame, perhaps the shame of an ambiguous gender identity, and if Paul continues to wear it, then the Pauline ethics announced by Fredrickson involve not the extinction of primary identifications, but of the cultural and institutional biases against them. Those who are perishing, in Paul, might be those who, in Fredrickson's Lutheran congregation, cannot bear the challenge of alterity, cannot bring themselves into community with people refusing to check their marginalized specificities at the door. Or even those who, closer to Paul's own day, refused alternative sexual identities such as Thecla's (see MacDonald 1983).

In a longer, more focused reception reading of this sort, I would want to spend a good deal more time tracing out the implications of (probably just a few of) the associative connections I have hinted at here. The goal would be similar, though, not to locate Hawthorne's biblical resources and consider them only in their own historical context—as useful as work like that can be (as in Conor Michael Walsh's unpublished 2009 dissertation *Nathaniel Hawthorne and His Biblical Contexts*; see also Courtmanche 2008)—but rather, by pursuing quite freely 'unorthodox combinations and transgressive juxtapositions of things normally kept apart' (Stone 2001: 31), to prompt unusual and challenging questions of Paul, to the extent that Paul is always our reading of Paul. In some cases, we may be led to read Paul differently, critically, through the lens of other texts, with a new awareness of problematic Pauline material that only seems benign. In other cases, we may find that Paul himself, when read slightly askew, questions the assumptions behind later perspectives developed in his name. The best historical- and literary-critical work can obviously do something similar, especially when a new understanding of Paul's language and context renders some consensus view less acceptable, or, at least, more complicated. The difference is that reception of the sort I have only sketched here is less invested in historical accuracy or authorial intent. The cultural and political work performed by readings of Paul is what matters. And how better to engage that work than by means of other readings, readings also engaging Paul, but from outside the biblical studies and theological mainstreams? If, as J. Hillis Miller notes, any one text is always liable to be beyond interpretation, then multiple texts in shifting contexts will simply refuse all the more to cohere around a single meaning, be it Paul's or our own.

BIBLIOGRAPHY

Adams, Edward, and David G. Horrell (eds.)
2004   *Christianity at Corinth: The Quest for the Pauline Church* (Louisville, KY: Westminster John Knox Press).

Ashton, John
2000   *The Religion of Paul the Apostle* (New Haven, CT: Yale University Press).

Aus, Roger David
2005   *Imagery of Triumph and Rebellion in 2 Corinthians 2:14-17 and Elsewhere in the Epistle: An Example of the Combination of Greco-Roman and Judaic Traditions in the Apostle Paul* (Studies in Judaism; Lanham, MD: University Press of America).

Badiou, Alain
1997   *Saint Paul: The Foundation of Universalism* (Cultural Memory in the Present; Stanford, CA: Stanford University Press).

Baird, William
1985   'Visions, Revelation, and Ministry: Reflections on 2 Cor. 12:1-5 and Gal. 1:11-17', *Journal of Biblical Literature* 104, pp. 651-62.

Bal, Mieke
2008   *Loving Yusuf: Conceptual Travels from Present to Past* (Afterlives of the Bible; Chicago: University of Chicago Press).

Barnett, Paul
1997   *The Second Epistle to the Corinthians* (NICNT; Grand Rapids, MI: Wm B. Eerdmans Publishing).

Barrett, C.K.
1973   *A Commentary on the Second Epistle to the Corinthians* (Black's New Testament Commentaries; London: Black).

Betz, Hans Dieter
1972   *Der Apostel Paulus und die sokratische Tradition: Eine exegetische Untersuchung zu seiner 'Apologie' 2 Korinther 10–13* (BHT, 45; Tübingen: J.C.B. Mohr).
1973   '2 Cor. 6:14–7:1: An Anti-Pauline Fragment?' *Journal of Biblical Literature* 92, pp. 88-108.

1985   *2 Corinthians 8 and 9: A Commentary on Two Administrative Letters of the*
        Apostle Paul (Hermeneia; Philadelphia, PA: Fortress Press).
2000   'The Concept of the "Inner Human Being" (*ho esō anthrōpos*) in the
        Anthropology of Paul', *New Testament Studies* 46, pp. 315-41.

Birk, John F.
1996   'Hawthorne's Mister Hooper: The Veil of Ham?' *Prospects* 21, pp. 1-11.

Blackburn, Barry
1991   *Theios Anēr and the Markan Miracle Traditions: A Critique of the Theios Anēr*
        Concept as an Interpretative Background of the Miracle Traditions Used by Mark
        (WUNT, 2/40; Tübingen: Mohr Siebeck).

Blanton, Thomas
2011   'Symbolic Goods as Media of Exchange in Paul's Gift Economy', Proceedings
        of the Society for the Study of Early Christianity. Accessible at http://
        www.mq.edu.au/about_us/faculties_and_departments/faculty_of_arts/
        department_of_ancient_history/community_partners/ssec/conference/
        proceedings_2011/.

Boer, Martinus C. de
2011   *Galatians* (The New Testament Library; Louisville, KY: Westminster John
        Knox Press).

Boer, Roland
1999   *Knockin' on Heaven's Door* (Biblical Limits; New York: Routledge).

Bormann, Lukas, Kelly Del Tredici and Angela Standhartinger (eds.)
1994   *Religious Propaganda and Missionary Competition in the New Testament World:*
        Essays Honoring Dieter Georgi (NovTSup, 74; Leiden: Brill).

Boyarin, Daniel
1997   *A Radical Jew: Paul and the Politics of Identity* (Contraversions, 1; Berkeley,
        CA: University of California Press).

Braxton, Brad R.
2008   'Paul and Racial Reconciliation: A Postcolonial Approach to 2 Corinthians
        3:12-18', in *Scripture and Traditions: Essays on Early Judaism and Christianity*
        in Honor of Carl R. Holladay (NovTSup, 129; ed. Patrick Gray and Gail R.
        O'Day; Leiden: Brill), pp. 411-28.

Britt, Brian M.
2004   *Rewriting Moses: The Narrative Eclipse of the Text* (JSOTSup, 402; New York:
        T. & T. Clark).

Bultmann, Rudolf Karl
2007 [1951]   *Theology of the New Testament*, I (Waco, TX: Baylor University
              Press).

Cameron, Ron, and Merrill P. Miller (eds.)
2011   *Redescribing Paul and the Corinthians* (Early Christianity and its Literature, 5; Atlanta, GA: Society of Biblical Literature).

Campbell, Douglas A.
2009   '2 Corinthians 4:13: Evidence in Paul That Christ Believes', *Journal of Biblical Literature* 128, pp. 337-56.

Castelli, Elizabeth Anne
1991   *Imitating Paul: A Discourse of Power* (Literary Currents in Biblical Interpretation; Louisville, KY: Westminster John Knox Press).

Channing, William Ellery
1836   *Slavery* (Boston, MA: J. Munroe & Company).

Childs, Brevard S.
2004   *The Book of Exodus: A Critical, Theological Commentary* (Old Testament Library; Louisville, KY: Westminster John Knox Press).

Colacurcio, Michael J.
1995   *The Province of Piety: Moral History in Hawthorne's Early Tales* (Durham, NC: Duke University Press).

Courtmanche, Jason Charles
2008   *How Nathaniel Hawthorne's Narratives are Shaped by Sin: His Use of Biblical Typology in his Four Major Works* (Lewiston, NY: Edwin Mellen Press).

Dickens, Charles
2007   *A Tale of Two Cities* (New York: Signet Classics).

DiMattei, Steven
2008   'Biblical Narratives', in Porter and Stanley, pp. 59-93.

Dodd, Charles Harold
1967   *New Testament Studies* (Manchester: Manchester University Press).

Downs, David J.
2008   *The Offering of the Gentiles: Paul's Collection for Jerusalem in its Chronological, Cultural, and Cultic Contexts* (WUNT, 2/248; Tübingen: Mohr Siebeck).

Duff, Paul B.
1991   'Metaphor, Motif, and Meaning: The Rhetorical Strategy behind the Image "Led in Triumph" in 2 Corinthians 2:14', *Catholic Biblical Quarterly* 53, pp. 79-92.
1993   'The Mind of the Redactor: 2 Cor. 6:14–7:1 in Its Secondary Context', *Novum Testamentum* 35, pp. 160-80.
2004   'Glory in the Ministry of Death: Gentile Condemnation and Letters of Recommendation in 2 Cor. 3:6-18', *Novum Testamentum* 46, pp. 313-37.

Dunn, James D.G.
2006 *The Theology of Paul the Apostle* (Grand Rapids, MI: Wm B. Eerdmans Publishing).

Dunne, Éamonn
2010 *J. Hillis Miller and the Possibilities of Reading: Literature after Deconstruction* (New York: Continuum).

Ehrensperger, Kathy
2009 *Paul and the Dynamics of Power: Communication and Interaction in the Early Christ-Movement* (LNTS, 325; New York: Continuum).

Equiano, Olaudah
2003 *The Interesting Narrative and Other Writings* (New York: Penguin Classics, rev. edn).

Fee, Gordon D.
2001 *To What End Exegesis? Essays Textual, Exegetical, and Theological* (Grand Rapids, MI: Wm B. Eerdmans Publishing).

Fitzmyer, Joseph A.
1993 *According to Paul: Studies in the Theology of the Apostle* (New York: Paulist Press).
2008 *First Corinthians: A New Translation with Introduction and Commentary* (Anchor Bible, 32; New Haven, CT: Yale University Press).

Fredrickson, David E.
1998 'Pauline Ethics: Congregations as Communities of Moral Deliberation', in *The Promise of Lutheran Ethics* (ed. Karen L. Bloomquist and John R. Stumme; Minneapolis, MN: Fortress Press), pp. 115-30.
2003 'Paul, Hardships, and Suffering', in *Paul in the Greco-Roman World: A Handbook* (ed. J. Paul Sampley; Harrisburg, PA: Trinity Press), pp. 172-97.

Frör, Hans
1995 *You Wretched Corinthians!* (trans. John Bowden; London: SCM Press).

Furnish, Victor Paul
1984 *II Corinthians* (Anchor Bible, 32A; New York: Doubleday).

Gaventa, Beverly Roberts
1999 'The Economy of Grace: Reflections on 2 Corinthians 8 and 9', in *Grace Upon Grace: Essays in Honor of Thomas A. Langford* (ed. Robert K. Johnston, L. Gregory Jones and Jonathan R. Wilson; Nashville, TN: Abingdon Press), pp. 51-62.

Georgi, Dieter
1986 *The Opponents of Paul in Second Corinthians* (Studies in the New Testament and its World; Philadelphia, PA: Fortress Press).

1991   *Theocracy in Paul's Praxis and Theology* (Minneapolis, MN: Fortress Press).

2005   *The City in the Valley: Biblical Interpretation and Urban Theology* (Studies in Biblical Literature, 7; Atlanta, GA: Society of Biblical Literature).

Given, Mark Douglas

2001   *Paul's True Rhetoric: Ambiguity, Cunning, and Deception in Greece and Rome* (Emory Studies in Early Christianity; New York: Continuum).

Glancy, Jennifer A.

2004   'Boasting of Beatings (2 Corinthians 11:23-25)', *Journal of Biblical Literature* 123, pp. 99-135.

2010   *Corporal Knowledge: Early Christian Bodies* (New York: Oxford University Press).

Gooder, Paula

2006   *Only the Third Heaven?:2 Corinthians 12.1-10 and Heavenly Ascent* (LNTS, 313; New York: Continuum).

Gunther, John J.

1973   *St Paul's Opponents and their Background: A Study of Apocalyptic and Jewish Sectarian Teachings* (NovTSup, 35; Leiden: Brill).

Hafemann, Scott J.

1986   *Suffering and the Spirit: An Exegetical Study of II Cor. 2:14–3:3 within the Context of the Corinthian Correspondence* (WUNT, 2/19; Tübingen: J.C.B. Mohr).

1996   *Paul, Moses, and the History of Israel: The Letter/Spirit Contrast and the Argument from Scripture in 2 Corinthians 3* (Peabody, MA: Hendrickson Publishers).

2000   *2 Corinthians* (NIV Application Commentary; Grand Rapids, MI: Zondervan).

Hall, David R.

2003   *The Unity of the Corinthian Correspondence* (JSNTSup, 251; New York: Continuum).

Harrill, James Albert

2006   *Slaves in the New Testament: Literary, Social, and Moral Dimensions* (Minneapolis, MN: Fortress Press).

Harris, Murray J.

2005   *The Second Epistle to the Corinthians: A Commentary on the Greek Text* (New International Greek Testament Commentary; Grand Rapids, MI: Wm B. Eerdmans Publishing).

Hawthorne, Nathaniel

1987   *Selected Tales and Sketches* (ed. Michael J. Colacurcio; New York: Penguin).

Hays, Richard B.
1993   *Echoes of Scripture in the Letters of Paul* (New Haven, CT: Yale University Press).

Hearon, Holly E.
2006   '1 and 2 Corinthians', in *The Queer Bible Commentary* (ed. Deryn Guest; London: SCM).

Holladay, Carl R.
1977   *THEIOS ANER in Hellenistic Judaism: A Critique of the Use of this Category in New Testament Christology* (SBLDS, 40; Missoula, MT: Scholars Press).

Hooker, Morna D.
1981   'Interchange and Suffering', in *Suffering and Martyrdom in the New Testament: Studies Presented to G.M. Styler* (ed. William Horbury; New York: Cambridge University Press), pp. 70-83.

Horrell, David G.
1996   *The Social Ethos of the Corinthian Correspondence: Interests and Ideology from 1 Corinthians to 1 Clement* (Studies of the New Testament and its World; New York: Continuum).

Horsley, Richard A.
2009   'The First and Second Letters to the Corinthians', in *Postcolonial Commentary on the New Testament Writings* (Bible and Postcolonialism; ed. Fernando F. Segovia and R.S. Sugirtharajah; New York: T. & T. Clark), pp. 222-30.

Hubbard, Moyer V.
2002   *New Creation in Paul's Letters and Thought* (SNTMS, 119; New York: Cambridge University Press).

Jackson, T. Ryan
2010   *New Creation in Paul's Letters: A Study of the Historical and Social Setting of a Pauline Concept* (WUNT, 2/272; Tübingen: Mohr Siebeck).

Jennings, Theodore W.
2006   *Reading Derrida/Thinking Paul: On Justice* (Cultural Memory in the Present; Stanford, CA: Stanford University Press).
2009   *Transforming Atonement: A Political Theology of the Cross* (Minneapolis, MN: Fortress Press).

Joubert, Stephan
2000   *Paul as Benefactor: Reciprocity, Strategy and Theological Reflection in Paul's Collection* (WUNT, 2/214; Tübingen: Mohr Siebeck).

Judge, E.A.
2008   *The First Christians in the Roman World: Augustan and New Testament Essays* (ed. James R. Harrison; WUNT, 229; Tübingen: Mohr Siebeck).

Kim, Seyoon
2002   *Paul and the New Perspective: Second Thoughts on the Origin of Paul's Gospel* (Grand Rapids, MI: Wm B. Eerdmans Publishing).

King, Martin Luther, Jr
1992   *I Have a Dream: Writings and Speeches That Changed the World* (New York: HarperCollins).
2007   'Unfulfilled Hopes', in *The Papers of Martin Luther King, Jr*, VI (ed. Clayborne Carson *et al.*; Berkeley, CA: University of California Press), pp. 359-67.

Kruse, Colin
2008   *2 Corinthians* (TNTC, 8; Downers Grove, IL: IVP Academic).

Larson, Jennifer
2004   'Paul's Masculinity', *Journal of Biblical Literature* 123, pp. 85-97.

Levine, Amy-Jill (ed.)
2004   *A Feminist Companion to Paul* (FCNT, 6; New York: T. & T. Clark International).

Lieb, Michael, Emma Mason, Jonathan Roberts, and Christopher Rowland (eds.)
2011   *The Oxford Handbook of the Reception History of the Bible* (New York: Oxford University Press).

Lim, Kar Yong
2009   '*The Sufferings of Christ Are Abundant in Us*' (2 Corinthians 1.5): A Narrative Dynamics Investigation of Paul's Sufferings in 2 Corinthians (LNTS, 399; New York: Continuum).

Lincoln, Andrew T.
2004   *Paradise Now and Not Yet: Studies in the Role of the Heavenly Dimension in Paul's Thought with Special Reference to his Eschatology* (SNTS, 43; New York: Cambridge University Press).

Long, Fredrick J.
2004   *Ancient Rhetoric and Paul's Apology: The Compositional Unity of 2 Corinthians* (SNTMS, 131; New York: Cambridge University Press).

Lowe, Matthew Forrest
2011   'Pleading and Power: The Missional Theopolitics of Paul's Ambassadorial Soteriology in 2 Corinthians 5:16-21'. Available at https://perswww.kuleuven.be/~u0007546/sbl/Lowe.pdf.

Lüdemann, Gerd
1984 *Paul, Apostle to the Gentiles: Studies in Chronology* (Philadelphia, PA: Fortress
      Press).

Luther, Martin
2005 *Martin Luther's Basic Theological Writings* (ed. Timothy F. Lull; Minneapolis,
      MN: Fortress Press, 2nd edn).

Lyons, George
1985 *Pauline Autobiography: Toward a New Understanding* (SBLDS, 73; Atlanta,
      GA: Scholars Press).

MacDonald, Dennis Ronald
1983 *The Legend and the Apostle: The Battle for Paul in Story and Canon* (Louisville,
      KY: Westminster John Knox Press).

Malherbe, Abraham J.
1983 'Antisthenes and Odysseus, and Paul at War', *Harvard Theological Review* 76,
      pp. 143-73.

Marchal, Joseph A.
2009 'Mimicry and Colonial Differences: Gender, Ethnicity, and Empire in the
      Interpretation of Pauline Imitation', in *Prejudice and Christian Beginnings:
      Investigating Race, Gender, and Ethnicity in Early Christian Studies* (ed. Laura
      Nasrallah and Elizabeth Schüssler Fiorenza; Minneapolis, MN: Fortress
      Press), pp. 101-27.

Marshall, Peter
1987 *Enmity in Corinth: Social Conventions in Paul's Relations with the Corinthians*
      (WUNT, 2/23; Tübingen: Mohr Siebeck).

Martin, Dale B.
1995 *The Corinthian Body* (New Haven: Yale University Press).

Martin, Ralph P.
1989 *Reconciliation: A Study of Paul's Theology* (New Foundations Theological
      Library Grand Rapids, MI: Academie Books, rev. edn).

Matera, Frank J.
2003 *II Corinthians: A Commentary* (New Testament Library; Louisville, KY:
      Westminster John Knox Press).

Matthews, Shelly
1997 '2 Corinthians', in *Searching the Scriptures* (ed. Elizabeth Schüssler Fiorenza
      and Shelly Matthews; New York: Crossroad), pp. 196-217.

2001 *First Converts: Rich Pagan Women and the Rhetoric of Mission in Early Judaism and Christianity* (Contraversions; Stanford, CA: Stanford University Press).

McCant, Jerry W.
1988 'Paul's Thorn of Rejected Apostleship', *New Testament Studies* 34, pp. 550-72.
1994 'Competing Pauline Eschatologies: An Exegetical Comparison of 1 Corinthians 15 and 2 Corinthians 5', *Wesleyan Theological Journal* 29, pp. 23-49.
1999 *2 Corinthians* (Readings, A New Biblical Commentary; Sheffield: Sheffield Academic Press).

McKay, K.L.
1995 'Observations on the Epistolary Aorist in 2 Corinthians', *Novum Testamentum* 37, pp. 154-58.

Meyer, Jason C.
2009 *The End of the Law: Mosaic Covenant in Pauline Theology* (NAC Studies in Bible and Theology, 6; Nashville, TN: B&H Publishing Group).

Miller, D.A.
1987 'The Administrator's Black Veil', *ADE Bulletin* 88, pp. 49-53.

Miller, J. Hillis
1991 *Hawthorne and History: Defacing It* (Bucknell Lectures in Literary Theory; Cambridge, MA: Blackwell).

Mills, Charles Wade, and Carole Pateman
2007 'Contract of Breach: Repairing the Racial Contract', in *Contract and Domination* (Cambridge: Polity Press), pp. 106-133.

Mitchell, Margaret M.
1991 *Paul and the Rhetoric of Reconciliation: An Exegetical Investigation of the Language and Composition of 1 Corinthians* (HUT, 28; Louisville, KY: Westminster John Knox Press).
2005 'Paul's Letters to Corinth: The Interpretive Intertwining of Literary and Historical Reconstruction', in *Urban Religion in Roman Corinth: Interdisciplinary Approaches* (ed. Daniel N. Schowalter and Steven J. Friesen (Harvard Theological Studies, 52; Cambridge, MA: Harvard Divinity School), pp. 307-38.
2010 *Paul, the Corinthians and the Birth of Christian Hermeneutics* (New York: Cambridge University Press).

Morray-Jones, C.R.A.
1993 'Paradise Revisited (2 Cor. 12:1-12): The Jewish Mystical Background of Paul's Apostolate', *Harvard Theological Review* 86, pp. 265-92.

Moss, Candida R.
2010   *The Other Christs: Imitating Jesus in Ancient Christian Ideologies of Martyrdom* (New York: Oxford University Press).

Munck, Johannes
1977   *Paul and the Salvation of Mankind* (trans. Frank Clarke; Atlanta, GA: John Knox Press).

Murphy-O'Connor, Jerome
1991   *The Theology of the Second Letter to the Corinthians: Jerome Murphy-O'Connor* (New Testament Theology; New York: Cambridge University Press).
1997   *Paul: A Critical Life* (New York: Oxford University Press).
2002   *St Paul's Corinth: Text and Archaeology* (Collegeville, MN: Liturgical Press).
2010   *Keys to Second Corinthians: Revisiting the Major Issues* (New York: Oxford University Press).

Nanos, Mark D.
2011   '"Judaizers"? "Pagan" Cults? Cynics?: Reconceptualizing the Concerns of Paul's Audience from the Polemics in Philippians 3:2, 18-19'. Available at http://www.marknanos.com/Cynics-In-Phil3-May11.pdf.

Niang, Aliou Cissé
2009   *Faith and Freedom in Galatia and Senegal: The Apostle Paul, Colonists and Sending Gods* (Biblical Interpretation, 97; Leiden: Brill).

Paget, James Carleton
2010   *Jews, Christians and Jewish Christians in Antiquity* (WUNT, 251; Tübingen: Mohr Siebeck).

Pascuzzi, Maria
2005   *First and Second Corinthians* (The New Collegeville Bible Commentary, New Testament, 7; Collegeville, MN: Liturgical Press).

Pedersen, Sigfred
2002   'Paul's Understanding of the Biblical Law', *Novum Testamentum* 44, pp. 1-34.

Person, Leland S.
2007   *The Cambridge Introduction to Nathaniel Hawthorne* (New York: Cambridge University Press).

Piper, John
2007   *The Future of Justification: A Response to N.T. Wright* (Wheaton, IL: Crossway Books).

Polaski, Sandra Hack
1999   *Paul and the Discourse of Power* (Gender, Culture, Theory, 8; The Biblical
        Seminar, 62; New York: Continuum).
2008   '2 Corinthians 12:1-10: Paul's Trauma', *Review and Expositor* 105,
        pp. 279-84.

Porter, Stanley E.
2005   *Paul and His Opponents* (Pauline Studies, 2; Leiden: Brill).

Porter, Stanley E., and Christopher D. Stanley (eds.)
2008   *As It Is Written: Studying Paul's Use of Scripture* (SBLSS, 50; Atlanta, GA:
        Society of Biblical Literature).

Potkay, Adam
1995   *Black Atlantic Writers of the Eighteenth Century: Living the New Exodus in
        England and the Americas* (New York: St Martin's Press).

Proudfoot, Merrill
1963   'Imitation or Realistic Participation: A Study of Paul's Concept of "Suffering
        with Christ"', *Interpretation* 17, pp. 140-60.

Punt, Jeremy
2008   'Paul and Postcolonial Hermeneutics: Marginality and/in Early Biblical
        Interpretation', in Porter and Stanley (2008), pp. 261-90.

Rawls, John
1971   *A Theory of Justice* (Cambridge, MA: Belknap Press).

Reid, Barbara E.
2007   *Taking up the Cross: New Testament Interpretations through Latina and Feminist
        Eyes* (Minneapolis, MN: Fortress Press).

Renan, Ernest
1869   *Saint Paul* (trans. Ingersoll Lockwood; New York: Carleton).

Rieger, Joerg
2007   *Christ and Empire: From Paul to Postcolonial Times* (Minneapolis, MN: Fortress
        Press).

Roetzel, Calvin J.
1999   *Paul: The Man and the Myth* (Studies on Personalities of the New Testament;
        New York: Continuum).
2007   *2 Corinthians* (Abingdon New Testament Commentaries; Nashville, TN:
        Abingdon Press).

2010   'The Language of War (2 Cor. 10:1-6) and the Language of Weakness (2
        Cor. 11:21b–13:10)', in *Violence, Scripture, and Textual Practice in Early
        Judaism and Christianity* (ed. Ra'anan S. Boustan, Alex P. Jassen, and Calvin
        J. Roetzel; Leiden: Brill), pp. 77-98.

Rudolph, David J.
2011   *A Jew to the Jews: Jewish Contours of Pauline Flexibility in 1 Corinthians 9:19-23*
        (WUNT, 2/304; Tübingen: Mohr Siebeck).

Runions, Erin
2003   *How Hysterical: Identification and Resistance in the Bible and Film* (Religion/
        Culture/Critique; New York: Palgrave Macmillan).

Savage, Timothy B.
2004   *Power through Weakness: Paul's Understanding of the Christian Ministry in 2
        Corinthians* (SNTMS, 86; New York: Cambridge University Press).

Schmithals, Walter
1971   *Gnosticism in Corinth: An Investigation of the Letters to the Corinthians* (trans.
        John E. Steely; Nashville, TN: Abingdon Press).

Scholer, David
2003   '1 Timothy 2:9-15 and the Place of Women in the Church's Ministry',
        in *A Feminist Companion to the Deutero-Pauline Epistles* (FCNT, 7; ed.
        Amy-Jill Levine and Marianne Blickenstaff; New York: Continuum),
        pp. 98-121.

Schussler Fiorenza, Elizabeth
2000   'Paul and the Politics of Interpretation', in *Paul and Politics: Ekklesia, Israel,
        Imperium, Interpretation* (ed. Richard A. Horsley; Harrisburg, PA: Trinity
        Press), pp. 40-57.
2007   *The Power of the Word: Scripture and the Rhetoric of Empire* (Minneapolis,
        MN: Fortress Press).
2011   *Transforming Vision: Explorations in Feminist Theology* (Minneapolis, MN:
        Fortress Press).

Schütz, John Howard
1975   *Paul and the Anatomy of Apostolic Authority* (SNTMS, 26; New York:
        Cambridge University Press).

Scott, James M.
1998   *2 Corinthians* (New International Bible Commentary; Peabody: Hendrickson
        Publishers).

Segal, Alan F.
1992   *Paul the Convert: The Apostolate and Apostasy of Saul the Pharisee* (New Haven,
        CT: Yale University Press).

Shantz, Colleen

2009   *Paul in Ecstasy: The Neurobiology of the Apostle's Life and Thought* (New York: Cambridge University Press).

Shaw, Graham

1983   *The Cost of Authority: Manipulation and Freedom in the New Testament* (London: SCM Press).

Sherwood, Yvonne

2000   *A Biblical Text and its Afterlives: The Survival of Jonah in Western Culture* (New York: Cambridge University Press).

Stanley, Christopher D.

2008   'Paul's "Use" of Scripture: Why the Audience Matters', in Porter and Stanley (2008), pp. 125-56.

Stegman, Thomas D.

2009   *Second Corinthians* (Catholic Commentary on Sacred Scriptures; Grand Rapids, MI: Baker Academic).

Stockhausen, Carol Kern

1989   *Moses' Veil and the Glory of the New Covenant: The Exegetical Substructure of II Cor. 3.1–4.6* (Analecta biblica, 116; Rome: Editrice Pontificio Istituto Biblico).

Stone, Ken

2001   *Queer Commentary and the Hebrew Bible* (JSOTSup, 334; New York: Continuum).

Stouck, David, and Janet Giltrow

1997   '"A Confused and Doubtful Sound of Voices": Ironic Contingencies in the Language of Hawthorne's Romances', in *The Modern Language Review* 92, pp. 559-72.

Stowers, Stanley K.

1990   '*Peri men gar* and the Integrity of 2 Cor. 8 and 9', in *Novum Testamentum* 32, pp. 340-48.

Sumney, Jerry L.

2005   'Studying Paul's Opponents: Advances and Challenges', in Porter and Stanley, pp. 7-58.

Theissen, Gerd

1987   *Psychological Aspects of Pauline Theology* (trans. John P. Galvin; Philadelphia, PA: Fortress Press).

Thrall, Margaret E.

1994   *A Critical and Exegetical Commentary on the Second Epistle to the Corinthians, I–VII* (ICC, 34; Edinburgh: T. & T. Clark).

2000   A Critical and Exegetical Commentary on the Second Epistle to the Corinthians, VIII–XIII (ICC, 34; Edinburgh: T. & T. Clark).

Vegge, Ivar
2008   2 Corinthians: A Letter about Reconciliation (WUNT, 2/239; Tübingen: Mohr Siebeck).

Walsh, Conor Michael
2009   Walsh, Conor Michael, Nathaniel Hawthorne and his Biblical Contexts. Accessible at http://digitalscholarship.unlv.edu/thesesdissertations/1115.

Walsh, Richard G.
2005   Finding St Paul in Film (New York: T. & T. Clark International).

Wan, Sze-Kar
2000   Power in Weakness: Conflict and Rhetoric in Paul's Second Letter to the Corinthians (New Testament in Context; New York: Continuum).

Ware, James Patrick
2005   The Mission of the Church in Paul's Letter to the Philippians in the Context of Ancient Judaism (NovTSup, 120; Leiden: Brill).

Welborn, Laurence L.
1995   'The Identification of 2 Corinthians 10–13 with the "Letter of Tears"', Novum Testamentum 37, pp. 138-53.
1999   'The Runaway Paul', Harvard Theological Review 92, pp. 115-63.
2005   Paul, the Fool of Christ: A Study of 1 Corinthians 1–4 in the Comic-Philosophic Tradition (JSNTSup, 239; New York: Continuum).

Westerholm, Stephen
2004   Perspectives Old and New on Paul: The "Lutheran" Paul and his Critics (Grand Rapids, MI: Wm B. Eerdmans Publishing).

Wimbush, Vincent L.
2012   White Men's Magic: Scripturalization as Slavery (New York: Oxford University Press).

Windisch, Hans
1924   Der zweite Korintherbrief (KEK, 6; Göttingen: Vandenhoeck & Ruprecht).

Winter, Bruce W.
2001   After Paul Left Corinth: The Influence of Secular Ethics and Social Change (Grand Rapids, MI: Wm B. Eerdmans Publishing).

Witherington, Ben
1995   Conflict and Community in Corinth: A Socio-Rhetorical Commentary on 1 and 2 Corinthians (Grand Rapids, MI: Wm B. Eerdmans Publishing).

Woodbridge, Paul
2003 'Time of Receipt of the Resurrection Body: A Pauline Inconsistency?', in
*Paul and the Corinthians: Studies on a Community in Conflict: Essays in Honour
of Margaret Thrall* (NovTSup, 109; ed. Trevor J. Burke and James Keith
Elliott; Leiden: Brill), pp. 241-59.

Wright, N.T.
2003 *The Resurrection of the Son of God* (Christian Origins and the Question of
God, 3; Minneapolis, MN: Fortress Press).
2009 *Justification: God's Plan and Paul's Vision* (Downers Grove, IL: InterVarsity
Press).

Young, Frances Margaret, and David F. Ford
1987 *Meaning and Truth in 2 Corinthians* (Biblical Foundations in Theology;
London: SPCK).

Žižek, Slavoj
2003 *The Puppet and the Dwarf: The Perverse Core of Christianity* (Short Circuits;
Cambridge, MA: MIT Press).

Index of Authors

INDEX OF SUBJECTS